LONGMAN IMPRINT BOOKS

Stories from

....

A range of modern sh   ....s

Selected and edited by Geoff Barton

General editor: Michael Marland
Series consultant: Geoff Barton

LONGMAN

Longman Imprint Books
General editor: Michael Marland

New titles
Characters from Pre-20th-Century Novels
Diaries and Letters
Highlights from 19th-Century Novels
Stories from Europe
Ten Short Plays selected and edited by Geoff Barton
Travel Writing
Genres selected and edited by Geoff Barton
Insights and Arguments
Landmarks selected and edited by Linda Marsh
Scenes from Plays
Stories from Africa
Two Centuries

Previously published titles
Autobiographies
Black Boy Richard Wright
Cider with Rosie Laurie Lee
The Diary of Anne Frank
Ghost Stories selected by Susan Hill
The Human Element and other stories Stan Barstow
I'm the King of the Castle Susan Hill
P'tang, Yang, Kipperbang and other TV plays Jack Rosenthal
A Roald Dahl Selection edited by Roy Blatchford
Stories from Asia
Strange Meeting Susan Hill
The Woman in Black Susan Hill

Contents

Modern fables

Introduction

When we embark upon reading a short story, we normally have a number of expectations. Most obviously we expect that, unlike a novel, it will be short. But there are other important elements which are traditionally associated with the short story form. For example, unlike a novel or play, characters are usually more lightly sketched. The central character often changes by the end of the tale – either by having learnt something, or being altered by some unexpected encounter. And short stories frequently move towards an unusual, even inexplicable ending which leaves us briefly baffled or dissatisfied whilst we think it through.

Stories from Europe illustrates the power and versatility of the short story form across Europe. Many of these key ingredients are present, but there is also an added sense of strangeness in many of the tales, with characters not behaving quite as we would predict, places seeming odd, and tales seeming to hint at other meanings. The moral for many of them, in fact, could be: 'Expect the unexpected.'

All but two of the stories (*The French Exchange* and *The Blue Jar*) were written in languages other than English. The American playwright Arthur Miller has discussed the process of translating literature. He takes the kind of active, creative role which perhaps only a well-known writer in his own right could. When working on producing an English version of Henrik Ibsen's play *An Enemy of the People*, Miller was concerned to use contemporary language. But since he could not speak or read Norwegian he had a problem. His solution was to have Ibsen's original text made into a basic word-for-word rendering. This gave him sentences like the following: 'Well, what do you say, Doctor? Don't you think it is high time that we stir a little life into the slackness and sloppiness of half-heartedness and cowardliness?' With his sure feel for modern American English, Miller used the language like putty, and the speech became: 'Well, what do you say to a little hypodermic for these fence-sitting deadheads?'

In this way, Ibsen's *An Enemy of the People* has become Arthur Miller's. In *Stories from Europe*, however, the translator's role is different. The best translators have an invisible role, taking the work of a writer and rendering it into English so that readers feel the power of the writer's original style rather than the ghostly presence of the translator. The best translations should probably not feel like translations at all.

So one important decision in compiling *Stories from Europe* was to seek translations which would allow readers to focus on the stories themselves, so that they would read them almost unaware that their original language was Spanish, Italian, and so on. If that proves to be the case when you read the book, then the true unsung heroes of the anthology are the stories' original translators. I hope that they, along with the study suggestions which follow, lead you to some lively and refreshing encounters with a host of Europe's most fascinating writers.

Geoff Barton

The French Exchange

by Penelope Lively

There would be the Kramers, Tony and Sue, in their Volvo and the Brands, Kevin and Lisa, in Lisa's new Sprite. And Dad had decided to take the Renault not the Cortina because the hatchback would be better with the picnic things. And the forecast was good. They would go to this prehistoric fort or whatever, anyway it was a hill with a view, Tony Kramer said it was a gorgeous spot. Sue was bringing some new quiche thing she was frightfully proud of and Lisa of course, inevitably, would be stacked to the eyeballs with the precious home-made sorbets. And Kevin was doing some sort of wine cup.

And oh, her mother went on, voice a notch higher, shouting up the stairs, isn't it a shame, Nick Kramer isn't coming after all. He's in France. On an exchange. The Kramers have got the Exchange so they're bringing him instead. He's your and Nick's age and he's called Jean something. Oh well, we'll just have to be nice.

She stood in front of her mirror. She heard her mother clatter back to the kitchen. It didn't matter about Nick Kramer; he was duff anyway. What did matter was that the new jeans quite definitely made her look fat. She took them off and put on the blue skirt instead but then the stripy T-shirt was wrong so she substituted the pink embroidered top with the low neck and suddenly her collar-bones looked enormous.

Deformed. She'd always known there was something wrong with her collar-bones, it didn't matter how much people she confidentially asked swore there wasn't. So the pink top was hopeless. That left the yellow shirt that made her look pasty, which was definitely out, so there was nothing for it but to start all over again with the jeans and the loose cream top that hid her bulge but made her bosom non-existent. And then her mother was shouting that they were here so in despair she had to stay like that and go down, bulging and bosom-less and discontented, and say hello to them all – Sue Kramer with tight white pants and one of those great baggy shirts and Lisa Brand in a short pink linen jacket and skirt thing and her hair done with silver highlights.

Hello, hello, they were all saying, and her mother was wondering if the barbecue stuffs should go in the Volvo not the Renault and her father was showing Kevin Brand the new ice-bucket. Hi there, Anna, Sue Kramer cried, Jean-Paul here's Mary and Clive Becket, and Anna, and the Brands you've already met, I say Kevin we were pursuing you all the way down the dual carriageway...

He wasn't very tall and he wore glasses and had spots. Copious spots. Not even remotely good-looking. Oh well. He inclined his head neatly, five times, and said '*Bonjour*'. 'English, Jean-Paul,' scolded Sue. 'You must *try*.' And Jean-Paul said 'Good day' and inclined again. But everyone was busy now arguing about who should go in which car and her father was looking at Kevin's this year's *AA Book of the Road* with a new bypass on it.

Eventually it was all sorted out. Jean-Paul would come in the Renault with them and the Kramers would take the barbecue stuff and follow and Kevin and Lisa would go on ahead because Lisa would want to go like the clappers once they were out of the speed limit.

He didn't say much. He got in the back beside her and said '*Pardon*' when their knees bumped and when her mother asked where he lived in France he told her and when her father asked if he was keen on sport he said no, perfectly politely. She took a look at him, sideways, without turning her head. Poor boy – it must be awful being so spotty. She could see half her own face in the driving-mirror; the new eye shadow was good, really good. Her mother was talking about Lisa and how she'd put on weight, did you notice, Anna? And then she remembered Jean-Paul and asked if he had any brothers and sisters and Jean-Paul said yes, he had one sister younger and one brother older, Solange and Stéphan, and that rather finished that off so her mother went back to Lisa and wondered if she'd like a copy of the *F-Plan Diet*.

South London thinned out and became Surrey towns all joined on each other and presently bits of country appeared and villages. Jean-Paul gazed out of the window. Once they passed a church and he turned, watching it recede. He said, '*C'est beau, ça.* It is of when?' 'That's a church,' said Anna's mother. 'Yes,' said Jean-Paul. 'Of what time, I ask.' 'Oh goodness,' said Anna's mother. 'I'm no good on that sort of thing.' '*Pardon*,' said Jean-Paul. He must be Catholic, Anna thought. She looked down and saw that he had awful shoes on, not the sort of thing people wear at all, but presumably they were French. She felt a bit sorry for him. The next time he looked her way she smiled brightly, to make up for the spots and the awful shoes, and he smiled back. His smile didn't somehow go with the rest of him; it was somehow detached, as though perhaps he didn't realise about the spots, or the shoes, or the peculiar way his hair grew at the back. Oh well.

Another village. A stretch of more open country. Jean-Paul leaned forward and said, 'Excuse. I wish the toilet please.'

Anna went crimson. How ghastly. Poor thing. Having to ask. If it had been her she'd have died rather, in someone else's car, people you didn't know. Actually Jean-Paul should have died rather, in fact. Waves of embarrassment and irritation came from the back of her parents' heads. Her father said, 'Oh . . . Yes . . . Sure thing. Soon as there's a likely spot, right?' And after another minute he pulled in at a lay-by beside a wood and the Kramers' Volvo pulled in behind and Jean-Paul got out and plunged off into the bushes.

Anna's mother sighed. 'I ask you! I mean, you can't tell a sixteen-year-old he should have been before we started.'

Sue Kramer appeared at the window. 'Sorry. But there it is – if Nick doesn't get his French O-level he'll have to take it again next year. Jean-Paul's been awfully little trouble, actually.' And she began to talk to Anna's mother about the holiday the Kramers were going to have in Portugal and presently Jean-Paul came out of the wood and got into the car and Sue went back to the Volvo and they all set off again.

Anna's cheeks still flamed. She slid a glance at Jean-Paul. He didn't, actually, seem embarrassed at all. He was looking out of the window and when they went through a place with a market square with old-looking houses he opened his mouth as though about to say something and then shut it again and smiled slightly, but to himself. Anna's cheeks went back to normal and she thought about their own holiday which would be in Greece and the awful problem was would she or would she not have lost five pounds by then and be able to feel absolutely all right in a bikini or would she have to spend all of every day on the beach holding her tummy in. None of the barbecue today, definitely none, and only a sliver of Sue Kramer's quiche.

Jean-Paul was saying something. She abandoned the bikini problem. 'Sorry?'

'I say, you should wear a hat of fur. Pretty – with black hair.' He gestured, circling her head, an odd, rather stylish gesture.

'A hat?' She stared, perplexed. Actually, her hair was very dark brown, not black.

'Karenina. Anna. For your name.'

'Oh.' She saw now; there was some Russian novel, the film had been on the telly once . 'Well . . . ' She laughed, awkwardly. 'It would be a bit hot, on a day like this.'

Jean-Paul looked at her attentively, and then shrugged. '*Tant pis.*' He gazed once more out of the window.

And now they were turning off on to the B-road that would take them to this hill and her mother was saying let's pray the charcoal lights properly, I felt such a fool last time with the Kramers, and oh God did I put the avocado dip in? Down lanes and through a village and round a corner and there was the red Sprite parked on the verge and the Brands sitting beside it on folding chairs like film directors use with LISA and KEVIN stencilled on the backs in big black letters.

There was a lot of shunting of cars to and fro to get them off the road and then a lot of unpacking and arranging of who would carry what and in the middle of it Anna's mother suddenly shrieked and pointed at the front of the Kramers' car.

'Tony! You got it! And we never even noticed!'

So everyone looked and now Anna too saw the number-plate: AJK 45.

'Oh, neat!' said Lisa. 'Your age too. I'm green with envy.'

'How much did that set you back?' asked Anna's father, and Tony Kramer grinned and said he wasn't telling. Jean-Paul was looking at Tony in a most odd way; he wasn't smiling but you felt he was somehow laughing. Everyone began to fuss round the picnic things and the folding chairs and the barbecue again and Jean-Paul said to Anna, 'Why?'

'Why what?'

He pointed at the number-plate.

He must be a bit slow on the uptake, she thought. 'It's his initials. And his age.'

'I know,' said Jean-Paul. 'But why?'

She couldn't think, when it came down to it. 'Well, it's a thing people do. There are lists in newspapers. Some of them are terribly expensive.' Actually her parents had been looking for ages for MRB or CTB but for some reason she decided not to say so. Jean-Paul gazed thoughtfully at Tony Kramer and said, '*Curieux.*'

'You're supposed to talk English,' said Anna sternly. He was four months younger than her, it had emerged.

'*D'accord,*' said Jean-Paul, and grinned. Really, his spots were the worst she'd ever seen.

There was a fuss going on now because Lisa had discovered she'd forgotten her sun-tan lotion and although Sue and Anna's mother had some they were the wrong kinds apparently, Lisa had to use this special one, but eventually she decided she might be able to manage with a hat, and they set off, through the gate and up the hill along a rough track.

Everyone was carrying something: the men quite loaded with chairs and loungers and barbecue equipment, the women more lightly burdened with picnic hampers and coolers and ice-buckets. Anna and Jean-Paul were at the back of the procession. Anna had her mother's basket with paper napkins and plastic cutlery and garlic bread in foil, Jean-Paul bore the bag of barbecue charcoal and Kevin Brand's wicker wine-bottle carrier with four bottles wrapped in tissue paper. He padded along a couple of paces behind her; the rest of them snaked ahead, calling out to each other, Lisa slipping and sliding on high-heeled sandals.

Jean-Paul said, 'Very serious – *le pique-nique.*'

She turned to look at him. Was he laughing? No, his expression was perfectly solemn. But something about his voice . . . Anna stared ahead at her laden parents, and their laden friends, at the glitter of chrome and the bright glow of plastic. She said – attack and defence together – 'Don't your parents do this kind of thing?'

'Ah yes. Absolutely. Also very serious.'

She felt, now, faintly uncomfortable. It was as though you were playing a game with someone you knew was much worse at it than you and suddenly they started doing things they shouldn't be able to.

'You enjoy yourself?' enquired Jean-Paul.

'Of course,' said Anna firmly. After a moment she added, 'Aren't you?'

'*Bien sûr,*' said Jean-Paul. He was, she saw, grinning hugely. He waved a hand at the landscape – 'It is beautiful day. The sun shines. All is agreeable.'

The track had petered out and they were walking on close-cropped turf up the hillside, which rose ahead of them in a series of bumpy terraces on which sheep grazed and small bright flowers grew. The leading group – Kevin and Lisa and Anna's father – had come to a halt and as the others caught up with them an argument arose about the appropriate point at which to pitch camp. Anna's mother wanted further on, at that flat place; Lisa wanted to be near a tree in case she needed some shade. Everyone disputed. Lisa said, 'Oh never mind me, I'll manage somehow, at a pinch I can go back to the car,' and Tony Kramer said, 'Oh no, we're not having that, love. Right then, the tree has it.' Kevin gave him a look that was sort of not quite as friendly as it might be and Anna's parents were telling each other that they needn't be so bossy in that joke-tone that, Anna knew, could topple over into not joking at all. And Sue Kramer wasn't joining in but gazed into the distance and tapped one toe on the grass.

Jean-Paul said to Anna, 'They enjoy themself too, do you think?' Anna, ruffled, pretended to be doing up her sandal. She was sweating after the climb and suddenly had the most ghastly feeling she might have forgotten to use any deodorant.

A decision, eventually, was made. Chairs, loungers, barbecue were disposed upon the bright grass. Lisa had loosened the heel of her shoe and Tony Kramer was trying to fix it with his natty miniature pliers on a key-chain and Sue Kramer was wishing loudly he'd get on with the fruit cup – everyone must be parched. Kevin was setting up the barbecue, in silence. Anna's mother was speaking to Anna's father in that bright, high voice that meant trouble.

The barbecue was lit. The fruit cup was made. Kebabs sizzled. Sue Kramer arranged herself on a lounger, gazed skywards and said, 'Bliss!' Glasses were filled. Birds sang. The spare ribs and the chicken joined the kebabs. Glasses were refilled. Anna's mother uttered an awful cry – 'Oh Christ, I've left the second barbecue sauce at home in the fridge!'

'Oh, for heaven's sake . . . ' said Anna's father.

There was a silence. 'But there's this delicious-looking one over here,' said Sue Kramer.

'But just the one!' cried Anna's mother. 'There should be a choice!'

'We'll manage,' said Kevin Brand. 'Forget it.'

'*Quelle horreur...*' said Jean-Paul, to the grass, shaking his head.

And now the kebabs were handed round on the gay paper plates, and the spare ribs and the chicken and the one sauce and the bright serviettes, two apiece – for lips and lap. And everyone was saying how brilliant of Tony to know about this gorgeous place.

'We are in the middle of a ... what is it? ... a field of battle?' asked Jean-Paul.

They all stared at him. 'Some sort of camp, I think,' said Tony. 'Prehistoric.'

'Or thereabouts,' said Lisa. There was general laughter. 'Now, now,' said Tony. 'It's not nice to make fun of other people's ignorance.' Lisa pulled a face at him and he aimed a spare rib at her, threateningly. 'Don't you dare!' cried Lisa. 'These pants are sheer hell to wash, I'll have you know.'

Jean-Paul watched, without expression. He turned to Anna and remarked, quietly, 'There is a tradition, then, of picnic here.'

'I suppose so,' muttered Anna. She had this feeling that everything was getting out of control – not least, in some odd way, Jean-Paul. There he was, with his spots and his awful shoes, and four months younger than her and yet you had this peculiar sense of him being somehow much older and floating above and beyond the spots and the shoes. She stroked her armpits, surreptitiously; she was sure there were visible sweat-marks on the cream top.

The quiche was being handed round now, and the salad, and the garlic bread, and more wine cup. Every-one was talking at once and Lisa Brand was shouting rather and Kevin was having an argument with Tony Kramer about something to do with the insides of cars, whether Tony's Volvo had a this or a that. Jean-Paul said to Anna, 'You interest in cars?'

'Not really,' said Anna, after a moment's hesitation.

'*Moi non plus,*' said Jean-Paul.

And now they were moving on to the dessert: the mousse and the sorbet and the little biscuity things Sue Kramer had brought. A different lot of gay paper plates; more bright plastic cutlery. There was debris all around now: heaps of plastic and paper and left-over food and bottles and glasses. A little way off a small posse of sheep stood gazing and chewing. 'Don't look now,' said Lisa, 'but we're being watched.' Tony Kramer laughed uproariously.

Anna glanced at Jean-Paul, but not so that he would notice. He was looking at some little orange butterflies that danced above the turf, and then his attention switched to a bird that hung in the sky just above the brow of the hill, its wings quivering. And then, as Kevin circulated again with the wine cup and a few drops got spilled on Lisa's white pants, causing distress, he observed that, in just the same grave and attentive way as he watched the butterflies and the bird.

The chatter decreased. Lisa was still dabbing at her pants, scowling. Kevin had wandered off a little distance and was lying on his back on the grass. Anna's mother was saying that of course it was heavenly here but what would be nice now would be a swim.

Jean-Paul rose, stowed his dirty plate, cutlery and napkin neatly in Anna's mother's basket and strolled away over the grass. He squatted down beside a clump of flowers.

Sue Kramer said to Anna, 'You are being so frightfully good with him. I'm afraid he's rather a dull boy, but there it is. Anyway, you're sweet.'

Anna smiled, embarrassed. Actually she'd never been

entirely sure she liked Sue Kramer. Nick Kramer she'd known since he was about three, and he was absolutely hopeless.

'And the acne...' said Lisa. 'One wants to simply pick them up and plunge them in some enormous vat of disinfectant, boys of that age.'

Anna looked towards Jean-Paul who, at that moment, glanced over his shoulder, caught her eye and waved. 'Look...' he called.

'Be nice, darling,' said Anna's mother.

There was a glinting coppery butterfly sitting on a plant, opening and closing its wings. Jean-Paul pointed, without speaking. Anna was at a loss; it was a bit odd, to put it bluntly, for a boy to be going on about a butterfly.

'A butterfly,' she said, with slight desperation.

'Yes,' said Jean-Paul. 'Of what kind?'

'I've no idea.'

'You are not interest in nature, either?'

'Well, quite,' said Anna (blushing now, curse it).

'I am interest,' said Jean-Paul, 'in astronomy, philosophy and the music of Mozart.'

Anna went rigid. Thank heavens at least the others hadn't heard him; they'd have died laughing. He was perfectly serious, that was the awful thing. What on earth could one say? He was gazing at her, reflectively.

'Tell me,' he went on. 'Why did your parents embarrass? About I need to go to the toilet from the car.'

She didn't know where to look. 'I don't know,' she muttered.

Jean-Paul laughed. 'Perhaps they are people who do not need to go to the toilet, never. *Formidable*!'

She looked back to the picnic group. Kevin Brand was still lying on the grass. Her parents were tidying up. Sue Kramer was sitting a little apart, reading a magazine. Lisa Brand and Tony Kramer were walking up the hill together; you could hear them laughing.

'I'm sorry,' said Jean-Paul. 'Now I make you embarrass too. I am not very nice. Shall we go for a walk?'

'All right,' said Anna. In the car, she remembered, she had smiled brilliantly at him to make up for his spots and his shoes.

They were round the flank of the hill, along the crest of one of the great ridges that lapped it. And Jean-Paul, incredibly, began to sing. She was afraid the others might hear. He sang this cheerful little song, the words of which she could not quite catch, and when they got to a point from which you could see great blue distances of landscape all around he stopped and waved at it and said '*Pas mal, alors?*' He was, she saw, perfectly happy.

She stared at him in surprise. There he was, this not at all nice-looking boy who wasn't tall enough, spending the day with lots of people he didn't know, most of whom hadn't spoken a word to him, and he was happy. It was ridiculous, really.

She said, 'Do you like staying with the Kramers?'

Jean-Paul shrugged. '*Ça va.* They are very kind. I must learn English for my examination.'

'Like Nick's got to get his French O-level.'

He grinned. 'So everybody inconveniences themself a little.'

They had reached the brow of the hill. Below them on one side was the picnic site, with Anna's parents and Kevin and Sue Kramer just as they had left them and on the other, sitting on the grass, were Tony Kramer and Lisa. Lisa's laugh floated up to them. And then suddenly she was flapping her hands around her head and there was a shriek and Tony was flapping his hands too and bending over her.

'*La pauvre dame,*' said Jean-Paul. 'She is bit, I think. A – how do you say it – *une guêpe.*'

'Wasp,' said Anna. She didn't feel all that sorry for Lisa Brand. Actually she thought Lisa had been going on rather, with her precious white pants and her jokes. Lisa and Tony were starting back up the hill now, Lisa with her hand clasped to her shoulder.

'Do you believe in God?' said Jean-Paul.

She looked at him in horror. 'I don't know.'

'*Moi – non.* Not since I am twelve years old. Because of he makes everything beautiful and then puts in the middle a wasp. Everything is nice and then – pouff! – a bus come and run over your mother.'

'Honestly?' said Anna, shocked.

'*Pas actuellement.* But it is what happen. *La souffrance.* So I do not think there can be anyone who make a world like that, or if there is he is bad and he is not God, because God is good. *Pas vrai?*'

Quite frankly, she'd never heard anyone talk like that in her life. You didn't know whether to laugh, or what. I mean, sitting on a hill talking about God. But there he was, doing it as though it were the most normal thing in the world.

Lisa and Tony passed them. Lisa was leaning on Tony's arm still clutching her shoulder. Tony waved and Lisa smiled bravely. Jean-Paul said, 'Perhaps that lady does not suffer so terrible. In the Middle Age people are roasting each other on fires and putting in hot oil.'

'Don't,' said Anna. She was hopeless at history, anyway; it was her worst subject, except maths. And this conversation was quite beyond her, out of control like everything on this stupid picnic. For two pins she'd have gone back to the others, except that in some peculiar way it had now become Jean-Paul who made decisions, not her. Just as, eerily, it was Jean-Paul who

13

seemed at ease in this place, on this hillside in a foreign country, rather than the rest of them.

He said, 'When I will be president of the Republic – no, when I will be king - king is more amusing, *tant pis pour la Révolution* – when I will be king there will be no earthquakes and no bad weather and I will give to everyone discs of the music of Mozart.' He looked at Anna. 'And what will you make, when you are queen?'

It was silly, this, really – I mean, if any of one's friends could hear... ' No more maths.'

'Ah. That is difficult for the banks and the shops and the men of business. Never mind, we arrange.'

She didn't know if she liked him or not. But more disconcerting was the fact that, so far as he was concerned, it quite evidently didn't matter. He wasn't bothered, one way or the other. And, maddeningly, it began to matter what he thought of her. Which was absurd...a boy like that. She tried to think of something to say that would be funny, or clever; nothing came.

'So that's where you've got to.' Her mother appeared suddenly behind them. 'Lisa's been stung by a wasp. The most unnecessary commotion, frankly. Tony's gone off to that village we came through to get some antihistamine. And someone left the top off the ice-bucket – wouldn't you know – so I can't do the iced tea.' She looked round irritably. 'I said all along we should have gone to the beach.'

'Where's Dad?'

'He's got one of his headaches, rather predictably. So Sue and I have been clearing up entirely on our own. Kevin's gone off in a huff.' She remembered Jean-Paul and said brightly, 'I'm so glad Anna's been looking after you.' She gave Anna a conspiratorial glance of sympathy. 'Anyway, I thought I'd better start rounding people up.'

They walked down the hill. Anna's mother told Jean-Paul that this was a frightfully pretty part of the country and Jean-Paul nodded politely and Anna's mother glanced at his shoes and his haircut and Anna knew what she was thinking. She wished she was somewhere else. She wished, particularly, that Jean-Paul was somewhere else but for her own sake rather than for his.

They reached the picnic place, where Anna's father, Lisa Brand, Kevin Brand and Sue Kramer were all sitting a little apart from each other and not saying anything. Lisa was holding a handkerchief to her neck and Anna's father had his eyes closed. And then Tony Kramer came panting up the hill waving a tube and Lisa cried, 'Oh, Tony, bless you – you really are an angel.' Kevin Brand picked up a newspaper and began to read it and Sue Kramer said, 'Sir Lancelot to the rescue,' and laughed in a not particularly amused way.

Anna's mother had just discovered she had trodden in a pile of sheep-muck and was hopping about with one of her new Russell & Bromley sandals off, trying to clean it.

Jean-Paul looked around at them all. He smiled benignly. He said, 'I wish to thank for you bring me to this charming place.' They all gazed at him in astonishment and he continued to smile benignly and sat down on the grass. 'I enjoy myself very much,' he said.

For a moment there was silence. Then Tony Kramer exclaimed heartily, 'And that goes for everyone, I imagine. Terrific outing. Sort of day that should go on for ever.'

'Absolutely,' murmured Lisa.

'Quite,' said Anna's father. 'Though alas we, I'm

afraid, will have to push off shortly.' He gave Anna's mother one of those looks that was not a look but an instruction and she scowled back and continued to rearrange picnic baskets and barbecue stuff.

They walked in procession down the hill. This time Jean-Paul led the way and was the most heavily burdened, having insisted on carrying the two loungers. Even so, he walked faster than anyone else; he was, Anna could hear, singing that little song again. No one else was saying much except Lisa who was telling Tony Kramer her neck felt heaps better now, entirely thanks to him.

The right possessions were stowed into the right cars. They told each other what a marvellous day it had been. Anna's mother kissed everyone and Sue Kramer kissed everyone except Lisa Brand, and Jean-Paul went round shaking hands. When he got to Anna he said, 'When I am king I make you minister of finance, OK?' and Anna went scarlet. Jean-Paul got in with the Kramers and Kevin and Lisa got into their Sprite and Anna got into the Renault with her parents. Engines started. Everyone waved.

Anna's mother said, 'What on earth was that boy saying?'

'Nothing.'

'Did you manage to find something to talk to him about?'

'Sort of,' said Anna distantly.

There was a grass-stain on her new jeans and she had eaten not one small slice of quiche but two helpings of everything so she would have put on about three pounds. But all that was the least of it.

They travelled back along the same roads but she did not feel the same at all. Ahead of them was the Kramer's car and through the rear window she could see Jean-Paul's head, and that too was different, uncomfortably different; it spoke now not of spots and a ghastly haircut but of small coppery butterflies and conversation that embarrassed, that left you uncertain, as though you had peered through strange windows. Jean-Paul did not turn round and presently the Volvo was lost in traffic.

Cousin Rosa

by José María Merino

Forcing the key into the lock, my cousin used both hands to turn it. She pushed at the door, which grated open. The darkness rushed out at us, was contained on the threshold, and suddenly became flecked with streaks of brilliant sunlight.

'Come on in,' she said.

Inside, the mill was also built of unplastered stone. In the centre of the dark room lay the huge mass of the grindstone. The sound of the stream rose from deep within, endowing it with the mysterious air of a live object.

The only light in the room came from a tiny window with dusty panes. Some stairs led up to the loft. They were made from stone flags driven into the wall at one end and fixed at the other to a long wooden beam that rose diagonally from the floor supported on three posts.

With no landing of any kind, the stairs ended abruptly in front of a door, which my cousin now opened. At the sight of the bare timbers of the sloping tiled roof which ran the length of the loft, with the crossbeams holding up the wooden floor, I imagined I was being ushered into a cabin far removed in time and space from the reality of that moment: my uncle and aunt's village, this June afternoon, my cousin showing me what was to be my workplace. An open window set in the far wall offered glimpses of the river, its tree-lined bank, the hills beyond it and their violent contrasts of light and shade.

In the middle of this room stood a dark, almost black, table, and next to it a wicker chair.

'No one will disturb you here,' my cousin said.

From the moment I set foot in the village (gingerly, still stunned by the protracted bumpy ride on the open bus lined with wooden benches on which passengers, packages and chickens were all crammed together in the afternoon sun), I had understood that my cousin would rule with a rod of iron. After the customary kiss on both cheeks, the very first thing she said to me was:

'I hope you haven't forgotten your books.'

I didn't say a word. By way of reply, I half lifted the bundle dangling from my left shoulder. She took me to her house, where I was able to greet my uncle and aunt briefly and leave all my luggage apart from the books, before she hauled me off after her without any opportunity to rest. We walked along the main road until we left the last houses of the village behind us. Then my cousin led me down a narrow track lined by dense clusters of foliage, pierced here and there by sudden sunbeams teeming with dust and insects, until we reached the watermill. The atmosphere created in that late afternoon by the building, the river, and the landscape, engraved itself deeply on my mind despite my torpor.

'You'll be able to study here to your heart's content,' she added. 'And I'll test you every morning, after breakfast.'

My cousin succeeded in instilling fear into me in a way that not even Don Fulgencio himself had managed to do, despite all his fury when on Mondays he used Latin as a bludgeon to crush the hostility he imagined he saw in his students, and which seemed so to embitter his days.

The summer days were radiant even though the thick foliage filtered the sunlight and swathed the mill in a cool green shade. The room I studied in was filled not only with the constant noise of water (in itself a double sound, a high-pitched rushing of the river outside, combined with a deeper but softer murmur of the water under my feet, beneath the mill itself) but also with the song of thrushes, the lowing of cattle, the twitter of swifts and swallows, dogs barking, and every now and then a voice, which always fragmented and dispersed on the breeze before I could catch the words being said.

The summer days were radiant, and all the sounds evoked the completeness of something full and irreplaceable. And yet I grew to loathe them every bit as much as the dark days spent shut in the seminary,[1] or even more – there at least the tedious routine and tasks were shared with others, and misfortune was spread among us all, whereas here, in this solitude, I was all alone to suffer the strictures of my teacher.

I tried to spin things out over my morning bowl of milky coffee, but my cousin would have none of it.

'Come on, wake up, don't play the dummy.'

And she was a zealous examiner of everything I knew, checking each question with a scrupulous attention that even my tiny writing could not deflect.

For the first few days, I was caught up in a strange kind of lethargy that I sought to blame on the stupor of the journey, as well as an ill-defined but determined desire not to have to do anything. This made it hard, even physically, for me to concentrate on the pages of my books, which swam before my eyes. All this prevented me from responding to my cousin's questions

[1] college

with at least a modicum of dignity. She said nothing on the first day, or the second. On the third, she slammed the book shut and looked me sternly in the eye, her own face flashing with aversion and distaste.

She had small eyes that were hazel-coloured with streaks of gold and red. One of them was darker than the other. Her insistent stare, combined with this disparity, threw me even further into confusion.

'Listen, don't think you can make a fool out of me,' she said. 'If you carry on like this, you'll pack your things and go home. The first thing I'm going to do is to write to your father, this very afternoon.'

I imagine I must have turned pale. I could still almost feel the thrashing my father had given me round my head, my neck, and the beneath of my back.

'No, cousin,' I shouted in alarm. 'I'll study, I promise you I'll study. I don't know what's been wrong with me these past few days.'

My mother took fright at the beating. My father turned bright scarlet, and was gasping for breath.

'I'll kill you, you booby,'[2] he spluttered.

That same night he decided to send me to his brother's house so that my cousin Rosa, who was his god-daughter and a student teacher, could take me in hand. While I sobbed in bed and my brothers and sisters lay in terrified silence, I could hear him and my mother discussing all the details of a lengthy letter in which they were outlining my situation in the most dramatic terms: a school year full of absences, waywardness, and a steady worsening that had culminated in the catastrophe of failing several exams and a warning about my future from the headmaster.

I forced myself to study, elbows jammed on the table,

[2] idiot

painfully struggling against the repugnance I could feel in my whole body. I occasionally left off reading to go down to the millpond to relieve myself. It was only at those moments, when the stream of my piss was splashing the smooth surface of the water, setting up ripples and for a few seconds clouding the crystal clear view of the gravelly bottom of the pond, that I recovered a sense of the sweet gratuitousness of summer, which dragonflies and swallows crisscrossed so contentedly. As I finished, the memory of the book waiting for me up on the loft table fell across my mind like the blade of the guillotine must fall across the neck of its victims, forcing me into an immediate renunciation that was both absolute and irredeemable.

There never was such a lovely, full summer as that one, and I have never missed it so completely. I gradually became accustomed to the arduous days of study and examination, sunk in a state of stupefaction like that which galley slaves must have felt as they plied their oars day after day. Whenever I lifted my gaze and saw the hillside blazing with sunshine, the leaves on the trees shimmering in the gentle breeze, I realised I was condemned forever to contemplate paradise from outside the gates.

And yet as the days went by, my dogged determination made the routine of study a little easier, so that it became possible for me to pass my cousin's implacable examination each morning and yet still have some time free in the afternoons to gaze out at the landscape. That was how I saw her.

The first time it was only an instant: a female shape which I guessed to be that of my cousin flashed across the path in a patch clear of brambles and trees. A short while later, I heard a splash, as though someone had dived into the water.

The next afternoon I was on the alert, and although she again ran quickly by, this time I could clearly see it was my cousin. The splash which followed confirmed my suspicion that she must come to the river for a swim.

I began to feel a great curiosity to watch her bathing without being seen. I don't think there was any lasciviousness on my part in this (at that time, the delights of the flesh were still very vague and imprecise for me); it was more to wreak a kind of revenge. It seemed to me that by watching my cousin swimming without being aware of it, I would be somehow avenging myself for the strict authority she wielded over me at all times, and especially during her morning examinations.

That afternoon I was engrossed in imagining the details of my act of revolt; the following one I could scarcely glance at a book, such was my expectation of her appearance. When I saw her flit by, I ran down stealthily, found the path and followed it until I reached the reeds at the river's edge. I finally discovered the spot where my cousin had stripped off: her clothes lay carefully folded on the stump of a tree at whose base grew the fat golden-coloured dishes of some large fungi.

When I heard a loud splash I moved cautiously forward among the branches, expecting to catch sight of her in the part the noise had come from. But I saw nothing except the deserted stretch of water, disturbed only by the slight ripples of the current.

This unexpected emptiness baffled me, until another splash, this time down by the mill, made me realise that my cousin must have swum over in that direction. I was afraid she might discover me in my hiding-place, so I crept back along the path until I came to a spot where I could see the river clearly again.

From here there was no sign of my cousin either. In

the background the silent, ivy-covered mill, which I had never seen from this angle before, led me to think of myself, shut in behind the open window which now peered down on the dark, motionless mass of the building like an empty eyesocket.

The river swept on along one side of the mill, while the water of the millrace, darkened by the building's shadow, plunged underneath it as if swallowed by an enormous mouth. The sun was already so low that it had sunk behind the trees at the water's edge, and there was a bluish, almost violet glow in the air. I remember being overcome by an odd sense of fear, so strange was the atmosphere the whole place had taken on at that moment. Then I saw the trout.

It was right next to where the main current and the millrace divided, and it was huge. I had seen large trout in my own village: there was one they hauled out on a gaffe that weighed close on thirteen kilos. In the water it had not looked half the size of this one. For a split second I told myself (though in my heart of hearts I knew the truth) that it was simply a long, dark stone that I had not noticed before. But its unmistakable shape, which allowed the play of light underneath, and its immobility in which it was nonetheless possible to sense an incessant quivering, were conclusive proof that this was indeed a trout. The shallowness of the water made it look even more impressive.

I stared at it in rapt attention for many minutes, while the sky grew darker and darker. In the end, the trout suddenly swung round, and with a flick of its tailfin disappeared upstream like a streak of lightning.

That enormous trout became for me a distorted image of all my winter longings. During all the boredom of the seminary, whose nets I was caught in for the whole school year, I was filled with a nostalgia in which my home river and its trout played a large part. That year, my second at the seminary, the hypnotic routines which dragged on amidst the smell of stews, chunks of stale bread, and greasy marble tabletops, in chilly rooms and high dark corridors, through interminably dreary days that seemed exactly like purgatory, convinced me of the value of all I had lost. One of the greatest treasures stored in my memory was the days when I had gone fishing. Ever since I was a small boy, I had devoted myself to learning and trying out all the different ways of catching trout. Even before I could swim I could tickle them under stones, pursuing them relentlessly even if a water snake appeared. Later on, I learned to fish with a rod, and to prepare my own flies for my hooks, which despite my clumsy fingers proved successful in catching these beautiful, shimmering creatures.

This gigantic trout was therefore like the phantom of all those I had been unable to catch, but had dreamt of with such longing during those endless days in the seminary: outside it was winter, a weak sun lit the dusty courtyard, the stumpy, bare trees, the brick wall enclosure, but in my mind I painfully dreamt of that same day and hour back in my own village, close to the river. Now, at the height of this summer I was also being robbed of, the trout appeared like a mysterious sign: surely nobody could ever have seen the likes of it.

That night I went to sleep in a happy frame of mind, my imagination filled with the image of its huge dark flank, the sure flick of its tail, its swift but stately movement. It almost made up for all the afternoons spent in forced study, and the mornings of gruelling questions.

As soon as I saw the trout, I was determined to catch it. The two months in which I had been obliged to subdue my real appetites had succeeded in creating in me the previously unsuspected ability of keeping something alive in my imagination while still following the thread of abstruse academic topics. Faced with my cousin's tireless daily evaluation of my progress, I was able to maintain the same frenetic pace of the first days at the mill, but also to create a space in my mind which I could fill with my daydreams.

I now slipped my new idea into this context. I began, so surreptitiously that it was not even suspected, let alone discovered, to conjure away bits of line, hooks, and feathers from my uncle, and with the new patience I had learnt to acquire, I made up flies that seemed most like the larvae laid in those days.

I left my tackle tied firmly to the river bank in different spots I could see from my window. My cousin still came to bathe in the river, on the far side of the bend, and the trout swam downstream until it came to its usual resting-place.

Finally, one afternoon it took one of my lures. A loud splash heralded the capture. I had tied my hooks to strong bits of twine, which were fastened at the other end to tough cord. The trout took the fly right by its hiding place.

I rushed downstairs and without a second thought leapt into the water, which in that stretch did not come up any higher than my thighs. The trout's body slithered in my hands, and I was afraid I might lose it, until I managed to plunge my fingers into its gills. The fish was far stronger than I had expected, and succeeded in knocking me over. I have no idea how long we struggled, but I do remember that we rolled over and over in the water for quite a distance. I think it was only my intense excitement that saved me from having to let go of the fish, half-drowned as I was by all the thrashing about in the water. Eventually I dragged myself to the bank and with a great effort threw the trout out of the water. Both of us lay panting on the path.

Stretched there beside me, the trout seemed bigger than ever. It was beating its tail furiously, and gasping for air. All down its huge body, the markings shone like precious stones. I lay looking at it in wonder.

Suddenly a discovery brought me down to earth. The trout's eyes reminded me exactly of my cousin's. It seemed to me that like hers, the fish's eyes were of different colours and even had the same expression. I felt frightened. It was that blue, mysterious hour of the evening. The watermill looked like some huge animal lurking in ambush. The gasping trout was staring at me with my cousin Rosa's eyes.

I pulled out the hook and pushed it back into the water. For a while the trout hardly moved, but then it swam slowly off until it disappeared in the middle of the stream, which was getting darker and darker as the light faded.

When I got back to my uncle's, I wasn't the only one who had met with an accident: my cousin had got caught on some branches, and sported a bloody tear on her upper lip. My aunt scolded both of us. To ward off the pneumonia she forecast for me, she made me drink a glass of homemade brandy (which, after burning my throat, left me drowsily tipsy). She also tended my cousin's wound, taking her to task for her crazy habit of going for a bathe every day. The peroxide bubbled gently on my cousin's lip. She stared at me, but I wouldn't return her gaze.

That was the last time she bathed in the pool near the mill. Nor did I ever see the enormous trout again.

The Black Dog

by J. Bernlef

'There's a fire at Voorthuyzen's bakery on Main Street,' his father had said during breakfast. 'A large blazing fire,' he had added.

Half an hour later he shuffled back, his head lowered. His father had laughed at him. His mother had found it childish that he responded so angrily to his father's joke.

It was Saturday, the first of April. Secretly he had wished his father dead.

Now it was the second of April. You can forget a lot in twenty-four hours. He took the usual Sunday stroll with his father.

Behind the still-closed outdoor wooden swimming pool the sandy land stretched ruggedly towards the pale green back-dike. While he dodged through the holes and half-caved-in huts of unknown boys in search of possible treasures, his father whistled softly through his teeth and smoked a Players from a pale blue pack, his shiny black raincoat folded in four over his left arm, for he never trusted the weather report, especially not in April.

At the edge of the dike his father sat staring for a long time in the direction of the three chimney stacks of the electric plant while he, the son, watched the schools of nearly transparent sticklebacks and the scurrying of pitch-black water beetles at the foot of a ditch.

These were always the best hours of the week, all alone with his father, who now took off his glasses and wiped them with a chamois[1] cloth which he removed from a front compartment in his purse. As if he wanted to get a better look at the three upright brick-red chimneys of the power plant.

Sitting on top of the dike in clear weather you could even see the ships slowly sailing through the Connecting Canal on their way to the sea.

These were the best hours of the week because his father didn't do a thing, but just sat there silently and every now and then gave him a short wave whenever he, sitting in a hunched position, would look up from the side of the ditch. He listened to the shrill cries of the peewits and the seagulls in the pasture in front of him. A lightly spotted rabbit jumped clumsily through the short grass.

When his father had finished smoking another Player he made the usual gesture. Time to return. Actually it was only a short walk to the back-dike, but the town's last row of houses still seemed to be far away.

A large black dog ran towards them over the dunes of sand in enormous lopsided leaps. A Bouvier de Flandres. You could tell by the trimmed ears lying flat against his head.

The dog began to jump around them, barking wildly.

'Just keep on walking.' His father had barely finished the sentence before he had to use both hands to keep the raving dog at bay. Savagely, with his head shaking, the animal settled his jaws into the black raincoat.

Only now did he notice the flecks of foam flying out of his mouth, the yellowish glare in his eyes and the

---

[1] soft leather

unusual rigid manner in which the dog fixed his paws, jerking at a flap of the coat with all his might while his father frantically held on to it with both hands. Every now and then the dog's black body trembled as if it were undergoing an electric shock.

He looked around him. A bed spring, a smashed orange crate. Not a person in sight. Nobody who could see them here. Nobody to help his father.

Suddenly the dog let go of the coat. His father lost his balance, stumbled over backwards, and the dog immediately plunged towards him with a wide-open mouth full of foam and threads of bloody slime. Lying on the ground his father gave the dog such a kick with one of his black shoes that the dog tottered a few steps sideways and stood in a daze for a few moments, as if the blow had brought him to his senses.

Then the dog shook his pelt and bent down, the front paws spread out before him, snarling at the ground. His father had jumped up, the shredded raincoat still in his hands. His left hand was bleeding.

A Dodge hobbled over the sandy land loudly blowing its horn. For the first time he dared to do something. He ran towards the stub-nosed car, his thin boy's arms swaying above his head. Come here. Come here. The driver, a man with a thick bald head and red cheeks, leaned out of the lowered side window.

'That dog,' he shouted gasping and pointing. 'That dog is biting my father to death!'

The man appeared startled by his announcement and accelerated. The car lunged ahead. He ran after the car, which rode in a circle around his father and the dog twice. His father made a motion to the driver. The car then made an abrupt turn and joltingly disappeared in the direction of the main road. And the dog sprung up again with his mouth wide open.

'Go away,' his father screamed. 'Run. Go home. Hurry up.'

He had to. Without even looking he ran from his father who would now surely be bitten to death by the dog.

He began to cross the sandy land, through the Sunday streets, along parks and lampposts, along the closed front doors of friends' homes, the fence of the nursery school, the pharmacy with its brown bottles in the window.

His father, bitten to death by a black wolf-dog. Covered with foam and slime. Bleeding all over.

He ran crying with quivering lips. Everywhere sat silent people across from each other in bay windows.

Panting, he let himself fall against the door of his house. He pressed the bell without letting go. He leaned against the door with such force that when it was opened he slowly glided together with the door's panel into the hallway.

From the open space of the landing above he heard his mother's voice. Who was there? He stumbled up the stairs.

He couldn't utter a word, only shake his wailing head. His mother gathered him up. What is wrong? What had happened?

Finally he sat plopped down in one of the armchairs in the living-room. She went to the kitchen and came back with a wet wash cloth which she brusquely rubbed over his face.

'What happened exactly? Quiet down and tell me.'

He could only wail, his drawn-up knees pressed against his chest. She could not understand it. Only he knew what he had wished upon his father while walking back from the non-existent fire that Saturday morning.

'Daddy is dead.'

He hardly felt the hard lashing blow on his cheek. His head jerked to the side and bumped against the headrest. It was as if his insides were filling up with ice water. He vaguely heard doors slamming. Then it became silent. In front of him a striped blue wash cloth lay on the carpet.

He let his legs sink to the floor, stood up and walked to the window. The field in front of the door was deserted. Because it was Sunday there were no playing children to be seen. He stood high above the ground and looked out over the lot, the pastures, the canal and the rows of dully shining greenhouses in the distance.

'I'm never going on to the street again,' he said loudly.

He turned around. The chairs, the table, the piano, the light rug with the cheerful orange rectangles; he stood in a room that suddenly had nothing to do with home any more.

Filled with panic he leaped into the side room and grabbed the portrait on his father's desk. His father and mother, arm in arm and laughing, somewhere in a garden.

'That was made when you were not here yet.'

Then this could also be possible. That everything would continue as before, the room, the dike, his mother, the school, only his father was not there any more. A dog which grew ever bigger and blacker while his father got weaker and smaller until he completely disappeared.

He had thought of it first, then he had said it and now it had happened.

From a thin silver frame his father and mother smiled at him. From a time in which he had not existed.

Perhaps that was why he sat behind the desk as if turned

to stone, the photo pressed between both hands, when the door opened and he heard his father's voice. As if he still lived. He put the portrait down. With his eyes closed he turned around. He heard his father laughing. Only then did he dare to look.

One of his father's arms was in a white sling. He laughed and leaned with his good arm on the marble mantelshelf. He was really alive. Both of them lived, he and his father, at the same time.

The door opened yet again and his mother entered, a tray in her hands. A teapot, three white cups and three saucers. Three spoons, a sugar pot. He could not keep his eyes from these things.

They went to sit at the table, each at his own place. His father on the left, his mother to his right. Walls and furniture surrounded them. His mother poured the tea. A thin golden-yellow stream that softly splashed into the cups. All three of them stirred their teaspoons at the same time.

He sat at the head of the table peering at a stain on the wallpaper and suddenly everything came to him from the dark spot on the wall as if from out of a hole. The fire in the not burning bakery, the picture from the time he had not yet existed and his bitten-to-death living father, who patted his head with his free hand and said there was no reason to cry.

'They did away with him right away,' he heard his father say. 'One shot through the head and that was it.'

A Vendetta

by Guy de Maupassant

The widow of Paolo Saverini lived alone with her son in a tumbledown shack on the ramparts of Bonifacio.[1] The town, built on a projecting spur of the mountain and jutting out in places above the sea, looks out towards the lower-lying coast of Sardinia, across the intervening strait, which bristles with reefs. At its foot, on its land-facing side, circling it almost completely, runs a deep fault in the cliffs, like some gigantic passageway. This serves as its harbour. Where it ends the first houses begin. Through it, steering a long, circuitous course, come the small Italian and Sardinian fishing-boats and, once a fortnight, the asthmatic old steam-packet which provides a regular service to Ajaccio.

Against the white of the mountainside, the huddled houses show whiter still. Clinging to the rock high above the awesome channel, where few boats venture, they look like wild birds' nests. The wind, never still, scourges the sea and batters the bare, eroded coast, where the grass grows sparsely. It roars into the channel, lashing the land on either side. The patches of white foam surging round the black snags of the innumerable rocks which rise everywhere through the waves, look like tattered sails bobbing on the surface of the water.

[1] a town in southern Corsica

All three windows of the widow Saverini's house, which was built into the sheer side of the cliff, looked out across this wild, desolate vista.

She lived there alone, with her son, Antoine, and Spitfire, a large, gaunt bitch, a variety of sheep-dog, with a long, coarse coat. When the young man went hunting, he used her as his retriever.

One evening, after an argument, Antoine Saverini was foully murdered – basely done to death with one treacherous thrust of a knife by Nicolas Ravolati, who escaped to Sardinia the same night.

When his old mother saw the body of her son, which bystanders brought home to her, she did not weep but stood for some time, without moving, staring down at him; then, stretching out her wrinkled hand over his corpse, she swore that he would be avenged. She would not let anyone stay with her and shut herself up with the body and the howling dog. The animal went on howling. It stood at the foot of the bed with its head craning towards its master and its tail between its legs. It remained as still as the old woman, who now bent over her son's body with glazed eyes and wept large, silent tears as she looked at him.

Lying on his back, in his rough wool jacket, which was holed and torn over the chest, the young man looked as if he were asleep. But there was blood everywhere: on his shirt, which had been ripped open by onlookers who had done what they could for him, on his waistcoat, on his breeches, on his face and his hands. Clots of blood had congealed in his beard and hair.

The old woman began talking to him. At the sound of her voice, the dog stopped its howling.

'There, there, my own, my poor boy, he'll pay for this. Sleep now, sleep, you shall have your vengeance, do you

35

hear? Your ma swears it. And you know your ma is always as good as her word.'

And slowly she leaned forward and pressed her cold lips to his dead mouth.

Then Spitfire started howling again, a howl that was long, unvarying, harrowing, terrible.

The woman and the dog stayed where they were until morning.

Antoine Saverini was buried the next day. Soon the people of Bonifacio stopped talking about him.

He had left neither brothers nor close male cousins. so there was no one to pursue the vendetta. Only his mother, who was old, thought about it.

From dawn to dusk, she could make out a white speck on the coast on the other side of the strait. It was a tiny Sardinian village, Longosardo, where Corsican bandits hide up when the police get too close. They are virtually the only inhabitants of the place, which lies across the water from their own country, and there they stay until it is safe for them to return home and go back to the maquis. It was in this village, she knew, that Nicolas Ravolati had gone to ground.

All day long she would sit all alone at her window, staring out at the speck and dreaming of revenge. How was she to manage it by herself? She was not strong any more and had not long to live. But she had given her word, she had taken an oath over the body. She could not forget. She had no time for waiting. What could she do? She could not sleep at night; rest and peace of mind eluded her; stubbornly, she went on looking for a way. The dog dozed beside her. Sometimes, it would look up and howl into the distance. Ever since its master had died, it would often howl like this, as though it were calling to him, as though the spirit of this inconsolable dumb animal had also stored a memory which nothing could erase.

Then one night, just as Spitfire began to howl once more, an idea came to the old woman. It was vindictive and brutal, the idea of a primitive savage. She thought it over until morning. Then, getting up at first light, she went to church. There she prayed, lying full-length on the stone floor, prostrating herself before God, asking for his help and support, begging him to give her poor wasted body the strength she needed to avenge her son.

Then she went home. In her back yard there was a broken old barrel which she used for collecting rain-water from the roof. This she turned on its side, emptied, and secured to the ground with stakes and stones. When she had finished, she chained Spitfire in this makeshift kennel and went into her house.

For the rest of the day she paced restlessly around her room, never taking her eye off the Sardinian coast. The murderer was there, over the water.

All day long and all through the night, the dog howled. Next morning, the old woman put water in its dish but nothing else – no meat or bread.

That day went by. Spitfire, weak from hunger, slept. The next morning, its eyes were bright, its coat unkempt, and it jerked frantically on its chain.

And still the old woman gave it nothing to eat. The animal, crazed with hunger, went on barking, though now it was hoarse. Another night passed.

When the sun rose, the widow Saverini went round to her neighbour's and asked if they would let her have two trusses of straw. She took some old clothes which had once been her husband's and stuffed them with the straw so that they looked like a man's body.

She fixed a stake in the ground in front of Spitfire's kennel and tied the guy to it so that it looked like a real man standing up. Then she made a head for it out of old rags.

The dog stared at the straw man in surprise and, though it was ravenous, stopped barking.

The old woman went to the butcher's and bought a long string of black pudding. When she got home, she lit a woodfire in the yard next to the kennel and set the sausage to cook on it. Spitfire went wild, jumped up and down in a frenzy and foamed at the mouth, but never took its eyes off the pan. The smell of cooking went straight to its belly.

Then the old woman took the soggy, steaming mess and put it on the straw man, like a halter. She tied it on with string, taking her time, allowing the juices to soak in. When this was done, she untied the dog.

With one vicious bound, the animal went for the straw man's throat and began tearing it out with its front paws on the shoulders. It dropped on all fours with a piece of the sausage in its jaws, then leaped up again, sank its fangs into the string, bit off lumps of food, dropped to the ground again and jumped ravenously for more. It ripped the face to pieces with its teeth and reduced the whole neck to tatters.

The old woman watched, without moving or speaking, but there was a gleam in her eye. Then she tied the animal up again, gave it nothing to eat for another two days and then repeated the same strange drill.

For three months, she put it through its paces, training it to earn its dinner with its teeth. She stopped chaining the dog. But now she could set it on the straw man with a simple command.

She had trained it to savage it and tear it to pieces even when there was no food hidden inside the neck.

Afterwards, as a reward, she always gave it the rest of sausage she had cooked for it.

Whenever the dog saw the straw man, it stiffened, turned to its mistress, who hissed 'Get him!' and pointed with her finger.

When she judged the time was right, the widow Saverini went to confession one Sunday morning and took communion with ecstatic fervour. Then she dressed in men's clothes, so that she looked like any other old, ragged vagabond, and agreed a price with a Sardinian fisherman, who ferried her and her dog over the strait to the other side.

With her she had a large piece of sausage in a canvas bag. Spitfire had eaten nothing for two days. The old woman kept letting the dog smell the food to make it even more ravenous still.

They walked into Langosardo village. The old woman limped into a baker's and asked where Nicolas Ravolati lived. He had gone back to his old trade, which was carpentry. He was alone in the back of his shop. He was working.

The old woman pushed the door open and called: 'You there! Nicolas!'

He turned. The old woman untied her dog and cried: 'Get him! Tear him to pieces! Kill!'

The dog went for him in a frenzy and got him by the throat. The man locked his arms round it, struggled and wrestled it to the ground. For a few moments, he writhed, beating the floor with his heels, and then became still. Spitfire went on savaging his neck, tearing great strips off it.

Two neighbours who had been sitting on their doorsteps later recalled having distinctly seen a ragged old man leave the shop with a thin black dog. The dog had been eating something that was a dirty brown colour which its master gave it as they walked along.

By evening, the old woman was home again. That night she slept soundly.

Big Fish, Little Fish

by Italo Calvino

Zeffirino's father never got into bathing-dress. He stayed in rolled-up trousers and vest, with a white linen cap on his head, and never moved away from the rocks. He had a passion for limpets, the flat clams which stick to rocks and become with their very hard shells almost part of the stone. To prise them off Zeffirino's father used a knife, and every Sunday he would scrutinise the rocks on the headland one by one through his spectacled eyes. On he would go until his little basket was full of limpets; some he ate as soon as gathered, sucking the damp bitter pulp as if from a spoon; the rest he put into his basket. Every now and again he would raise his eyes, let them meander over the smooth sea and call out: 'Zeffirino! Where are you?'

Zeffirino spent whole afternoons in the water. They would go together as far as the point, then his father left him there and went straight off after his clams. Limpets were no attraction to Zeffirino, they were so motionless and stubborn; what interested him most were crabs, then octopuses, jelly-fish, and then eventually any kind of fish. In summer his hunts became ever more arduous and resourceful; and now there was not a boy of his age who was so good with an underwater gun as he. In water the types that go best are rather stocky, all lungs and muscle; and Zeffirino was growing up like that. Seen on land, holding his father's hand, he was one of those crop-haired, open-mouthed boys who need clouting to drive along; but in water he outdid everyone; underwater better still.

That day Zeffirino had managed to put together a complete gear for underwater fishing. The mask he already had from the year before, a present from his grandmother; a girl cousin with small feet lent him the flippers; the gun he had taken from his uncle's home without saying anything and told his father they had lent it. Anyway he was a careful little boy, who knew how to use and take care of everything and could be trusted with a loan of them.

The sea was lovely, so clear. Zeffirino said 'Yes, Dad' to all his father's advice and went into the water. With that glass snout and that breathing tube, his legs ending like a fish's, his hands gripping that weapon, part spear, part gun, and part fork, he no longer looked like a human being. But as soon as he was in the sea, though he slipped along half-submerged, one could see it was him at once; from the shove he gave with his flippers, the way his gun jutted under his arm, the care he took to move along with head down on the surface of the water.

At first the sea-bed was of pebbles, then of rocks, some bare and corroded, others bearded with thick brown seaweed. From every fold of rock, or between the quivering beards of weed poised in the current, there might suddenly appear a big fish; behind the glass of his mask Zeffirino moved around anxious attentive eyes.

A sea-bed is lovely the first time when one discovers it; but it's lovelier afterwards like everything else, when one gets to learn all about it, stroke by stroke. One seems to be drinking them, these marine landscapes; on and on one goes and might go on for ever. The glass of the mask is a huge single eye to swallow up shadows and colours. Now the dark ended and he was out of that boulder-strewn part; on the sand of the bottom could be made out fine crinkles drawn by the move-ment of the sea. The sun's rays reached right down with peering gleams amid twinkling shoals of tiny fish swimming along in a straight line then suddenly all turning together at a right angle.

A little cloud of sand went up from the blow of a sea-bream's tail on the bottom. It had not noticed that harpoon pointing at it. Zeffirino was now swimming right underwater; and the bream, after a few distracted movements of its striped sides, all of a sudden rushed away closer to the surface. Fish and fisherman went swimming off between rocks bristling with sea-urchins until they reached a cove of porous, almost bare rock. 'Here it won't give me the slip,' thought Zeffirino; and at that moment the bream vanished. From holes and cavities rose a row of air bubbles which quickly stopped and started again elsewhere; sea-anemones gleamed in expectation. The bream peeped out of one hole, vanished into another and reappeared again at once from a distant aperture. It tacked along a spur of rock, headed down and Zeffirino saw a patch of luminous green towards the sea-bed. The fish lost itself in that light, and Zeffirino went after it.

He crossed a low arch at the foot of the rock and again had above him high sea and sky. Shadows of clear stone surrounded the sea-bed all round lowering into a half-submerged rock towards the open sea. With a thrust of his loins and a shove at his flippers Zeffirino re-emerged to breathe. The air-tube surfaced, away blew some drops filtered into the mask; but the boy's head stayed in the water. He had found the sea-bream again; in fact two! Just as he was aiming he saw a whole squadron of them navigating calmly to the left, and another shoal gleaming to his right. The place was swarming with fish, almost an enclosed lake, and wherever Zeffirino looked he met a frisking of narrow fins and a gleaming of scales. Between amazement and delight he did not let off a single shot.

He must not hurry, must calculate the. best shots without sowing terror around. Zeffirino, still with head underwater, moved towards the nearest rock; and in the water, along the wall, he saw a white hand dangling. The sea was motionless; concentric circles were widening as if from a drop of rain on the tense, terse surface. The boy raised his head and looked. Face downwards on the edge of the rock was a fat woman in a bathing-dress taking the sun. And crying. The drops came down her cheeks one after the other and fell into the sea.

Zeffirino raised his mask on to his forehead and said 'Excuse me.'

The fat woman said, 'Of course, boy,' and went on crying. 'Do please go on fishing.'

'It's full of fish, this place is,' he explained. 'Have you seen how many there are?'

The fat woman lay with face raised, her eyes staring ahead full of tears. 'I haven't really looked. How can I? I just can't manage to stop crying.'

Zeffirino was at his best in matters of sea and fishes; but in the presence of people he took on that stuttering open-mouthed air of his again.

'I'm sorry, signora...' and he would have turned back to his breams; but a fat woman crying was such an unusual sight that he stayed there spellbound, gazing at her in spite of himself.

'I'm not a signora, boy,' said the fat woman in that noble rather nasal voice of hers. 'Call me Signorina. Signorina De Magistris. And what's your name?'

'Zeffirino.'

'Fine, Zeffirino. Have you had a good fish? Or a good hunt? What do they call it?'

'I don't know what they call it. I haven't caught anything yet. But this is a good place here.'

'Be careful with that gun, though. Not for my sake, poor little me. But for your own, not to hurt yourself.'

Zeffirino assured her that she need not worry. He sat down on the rock next to her and watched her crying for a bit. There were moments in which she seemed to be stopping; then she would breathe through her reddened nose, raising and shaking her head. But meanwhile in the corners of her eyes and under her lids a bubble of tears seemed to be swelling up and her eye quickly overflowed.

Zeffirino didn't know quite what to think. To see a signorina crying like that wrung his heart. But how could one be sad facing that marine pen brimful of every variety of fish, and filling his heart with joy and longing? As to plunging into that green water and going after the fish, how could one do that with a grown-up in tears nearby? At the same moment, at the same place, coexisted two opposite, irreconcilable urges. Zeffirino could not manage to think of both together; nor of letting himself go to one or the other.

'Signorina,' he asked.

'Yes?'

'Why are you crying?'

'Because I'm crossed in love.'

'Ah!'

'You can't understand, you're only a boy.'

'Would you like to try and swim with the mask?'

'Thank you, I'd love to. Is it nice?'

'It's the nicest thing ever.'

Signorina De Magistris got up and buttoned the straps of her bathing-dress on her back. Zeffirino gave

45

her the mask and explained carefully how to put it on. She moved her head a little with the mask over her face, part-joking and part-coy, but through the glass could be seen her eyes which never stopped crying. She went into the sea gracelessly, like a seal, and began to hold her face down gaspingly.

Zeffirino, gun under arm, jumped in and swam too.

'Tell me when you see a fish,' he called to Signorina De Magistris. In water he never joked; coming to fish with him was a privilege he rarely conceded.

But the signorina raised her head and shook it. The glass had gone opaque and her features were not to be seen any more. She took off the mask. 'I can't see a thing,' she said, 'the tears are dulling the glass. I can't do it. Sorry.' And she remained there in the water, weeping.

'What a mess,' said Zeffirino. He had no half-potato with him to rub on the glass and make it come clear again, but did the best he could with a little saliva, then put on the mask himself. 'Watch how I do it,' he said to the fat woman. And they moved on together over that sea, he all flippers with his head down, she swimming sidestroke, with one arm out and the other folded, and her head bitterly erect and inconsolable.

She swam badly, did Signorina De Magistris, all on one side, with clumsy sweeping strokes. And beneath her for yards and yards fishes coursed the sea, star-fish and cuttlefish navigated, the mouths of sea-anemones opened. Now Zeffirino's eyes met seascapes that were quite bewildering. The tide was high and the sandy bottom was scattered with little rocks among which swayed clumps of seaweed moving to the faint movement of the sea. But looked at from above on that uniform stretch of sand it was the rocks that seemed to be waving about amid the still water dense with seaweed.

Suddenly Signorina De Magistris saw him vanish with head down, surface a second with his behind, then with the flippers, and then his clear shadow was underwater, swooping down towards the sea-bed. When the bass noticed the danger it was too late; the loosed harpoon had already hit it aslant and the middle prong was stuck near its tail, piercing right through. The bass straightened its spiky fins and rushed off beating the water, the other prongs of the harpoon had not hit it and it still hoped to escape at the cost of shedding its tail. But all it gained was to impale a fin on one of the free prongs, and it was lost. The reel was already pulling in its cord, and the pink, pleased shadow of Zeffirino was above.

The harpoon appeared out of the water with the bass skewered on it, then the boy's arm, then his masked head and a gurgle of water from the barrel. And Zeffirino uncovered his face. 'D'you see what a fine one? D'you see, signorina?' The bass was a big silvery black one. But the woman went on crying.

Zeffirino clambered on to the top of a rock; Signorina De Magistris followed with some difficulty. To keep the fish fresh the boy chose a little rock-pool full of water, and they crouched down by it. Zeffirino watched the changing colours of the bass, stroked its scales and wanted Signorina De Magistris to imitate him.

'D'you see what a fine one? D'you see how it pricks?' When he thought that there was a faint interest in the fish leavening the fat woman's misery, he said, 'I'll just try a moment and see if I can catch another.' In full harness he dived.

The woman stayed with the fish. And she discovered that never had a fish been so unhappy. She began passing her fingers on its ring-like mouth, its gills, its tail; and now all over its lovely silvery body she saw

47

thousands of tiny perforations. Water fleas, minute parasites of fish, had become masters of the bass for some time and were gnawing their way into its flesh.

Ignorant of all this, Zeffirino now re-emerged with a sea-perch on his harpoon, and proffered it to Signorina De Magistris. So the two had already divided tasks; she took the fish from the harpoon and put it to keep cool in the rock-pool; and Zeffirino again plunged in head-first to catch another. Before he did so he looked every time to see if Signorina De Magistris had stopped crying; if she did not stop at sight of a bass or a sea-perch, what on earth could ever console her?

Golden stripes went across the sides of the sea-perch. Two rows of fins went up its back. And in the gap between these fins the signorina saw a deep narrow wound that had been there before the harpoon's. A seagull's beak must have bitten into the fish's back so sharply that she could not understand why it had not been killed. Who knows how long the perch had taken this agony about with it?

Faster than Zeffirino's harpoon, a bream fell on a shoal of little uncertain whitebait. It was just in time to swallow a whitebait before the harpoon was embedded in its throat. Never had Zeffirino made such a good shot.

'It's an outsize dentex[1]!' he cried, taking off his mask. 'I was following the whitebait! It'd swallowed one and I ...' and he explained the scene, showing his excitement by his stutter. No bigger or finer fish was possible to catch; and Zeffirino would have liked Signorina De Magistris to take part in his pleasure at last. She looked at the plump silvery body, that throat which had just a moment before swallowed the greenish little fish and

---

[1] large fish with big teeth and powerful jaws

been in its turn torn to shreds by the harpoon's teeth. Such was life in the entire sea.

Zeffirino fished out yet a grey rock-fish and a red rock-fish, a bream with yellow stripes, a fat dory and a flat bogue; even a hairy and prickly flying fish. But in each of them, apart from harpoon wounds, Signorina De Magistris found the pricks of fleas that had gnawed at them, or the mark of an unknown disease, or a fish-hook stuck in its gullet some time ago. That cove discovered by the boy, where every sort of fish met, was perhaps a refuge for creatures condemned to a long death agony, a marine hospital, an arena for desperate duels.

Zeffirino was now manoeuvring among the rocks. Octopuses! He had discovered a colony hidden at the foot of a boulder. The harpoon had already surfaced a big lilac octopus, its wounds dripping with liquid like watered ink; and a strange anguish now came over Signorina De Magistris. To hold the octopus a separate rock-pool was found and Zeffirino felt like staying there for ever, lost in admiration of the grey-pink skin slowly changing colour. It was also late and the boy was beginning to get a little goose-flesh, his bathe had been so long. But Zeffirino was certainly not one to renounce a family of octopuses already discovered.

The signorina was examining the octopus, its slimy flesh, the mouths of the suckers, the reddish almost liquid eye. And the octopus seemed to her the only one among the creatures fished up to be without a mark or sign of torment. Its tentacles of almost human pink, so soft and sinuous and full of secret suckers, made her think of health and life; some torpid contraction was still making them turn with a slight dilation of the suckers. Signorina De Magistris's hand sketched a caress above the coils of the octopus and she moved her fingers imitating its contractions, getting closer and closer until she grazed it.

Evening was coming down, a wave beginning to beat in the sea. The tentacles vibrated in the air like whips, and suddenly the octopus was clinging tight with all its strength to Signorina De Magistris's arm. Standing on the rock as if trying to escape from her own imprisoned arm, she let out a cry which sounded like, 'The octopus! He's tearing me to bits!'

Zeffirino, who had just that second managed to dislodge a cuttlefish, put his head out of the water and saw the fat woman with one of the octopus's tentacles reaching from her arm to take her by the throat. He heard the end of her cry too; it was a high and continuous howl but – so the boy thought – without a sob.

Up rushed a man armed with a knife and began slashing blows down on the octopus's eye; he cut off its head almost clean. It was Zeffirino's father, who had filled his basket with clams and was coming along the rocks to look for his son. Hearing the shout, and adjusting his spectacles, he had seen the woman and rushed to her help with the knife he used for clams. The tentacles went flabby at once; Signorina De Magistris swooned.

When she came to herself she found the octopus cut in pieces: Zeffirino and his father gave it to her to fry. It was evening and Zeffirino had put on his vest. The father explained with precise gestures how to make a good fry-up of octopus. Zeffirino looked at her and a number of times thought she was on the very point of starting again; but no, not even one tear came out.

The White Woman

by Arthur van Schendel

In a small town with little canals and tall elm trees lived a man who for his entire life had only observed people without having anything to do with them. It was said that he was timid, not a philanthropist[1] although he always subscribed to good causes. Never had he had any other pastime than books and reading; from morning till night, year in, year out, he had long reposed in worlds far from this one. Otherwise he was ordinary – no criticism implied – and the two old servants who had known him from his birth lived contentedly in his house. By day and by night he was in his room with the books, occasionally looking out at one of the windows at the back on to the garden, occasionally at one of the windows at the front on to the canal.

One evening at the window he saw black clouds scurrying in the dark; bare branches were being tugged at and the lantern light on the bridge moved up and down. It was chill; he smelled hail. He drew the curtains; he heard the swishing of the branches outside. Seated near the lamp he opened a book on stars, a page full of figures, numbers without end. And he read:

A white woman, on the eve of Spring, sat in the half light of birch trees on a hill by the sea. The trees were motionless. A light flickered in the sky, the sea lay down below in the mist: not a murmur. Beside each tree a

---

[1] a person devoted to doing good

strand of vapour rose up, a shape with its arms crossed in front of the head. The strands entwined, the shapes moved from one tree to the next. The leaves rustled, the vapours trembled, a glistening descended. Down below by the sea a voice cried out, a form stood there, a wave flopped on to the beach. The white woman held her hands in front of her face and descended. Then it was night and black and nothing could be heard except for a wave breaking.

His hands were stiff, his feet cold. He had the feeling that there was ice in the room, strange at this time of year. And casting up his gaze from the page beneath the lamplight he discerned the white in front of the curtain of one of the rear windows; he only saw the white of a garment and of a foot stretched out in front. And when another foot had appeared he straightened up and saw the figure had approached to where the lamplight fell. He knew this was no human being, no woman. He rose up and saw the face but, because of the moisture before his eyes, he was only able to discern something deep and dark swathed in white as white as snow. She drew closer and she raised a hand; he heard a voice and at this sound he felt the warmth of tears.

The time has not yet come, she said, perhaps later, then shall the time be. She sat down on the floor in the light of the lamp, hands folded in her lap.

He was a modest man, he dared not ask who she was and whence she had come. But the darkness of her eyes opened to him so he could understand all that she said, and though tears still slid down his cheeks he sat quietly at the sound of her voice.

You hear that I can speak, hence I must be an 'I' like every other creature but it has been a long time since I have known this. I also have memories of a time long before this, when I existed I don't know where. Perhaps it was the place of sorrows for when I think of this from a distance I hear sighing, moaning, weeping, everywhere around, as if multitudes throng and plead in the darkness and one voice sounds that might be mine. In the silences I have heard so much weeping that the thing I long for most is that sound. And at times I have thought why – thoughts without end and worse than all the weeping. Without those thoughts I could never have believed that I might be a human being, not here, no, not here or there, a human being who must be or who has been. Then I see an image before my eyes and it is as if the sun begins; I no longer ask whether it's true or not. I cannot speak of this, that once I may have been a human being, cast out young from mankind and always yearning, always hearing the crying, crying here, crying there, crying within my innermost being.

Her voice became high and plaintive: Why is it that it is so cold here? Tomorrow I must be here, then shall the time be, why so cold?

She rose and had rapidly disappeared in the darkness of the curtain.

Then he heard feet on the steps of the stairs: the maidservants were going to bed. He opened the curtain at the front, saw a hailstone strike the window, the black branches swishing in front of the lantern, but his vision was blurred by the tears in his eyes.

And again in the evening he sat beneath the lamp with his head bent over the book, reading about stars, their courses and distances. And again he suddenly felt the cold to be present there, and casting up his gaze he again saw the whiteness in front of the dark wall. The figure approached more rapidly and when she was sitting he made out the whiteness of the hands and the feet; they seemed hard yet without weight, white as hail without a sheen. She spoke: Dusk is where I have been waiting and no sheen can be there. We acquire sheen when we touch something, something standing on a foundation, here or yonder. The thought has asked whether this is why all the weeping must be. I know I long to touch the world and people but from the depths I must weep that this should happen. Why the fear? We both know that we cry and hear crying everywhere and that we all wish to come. We know the one cannot be without the other and that there must be pain when two meet together. Not two dust specks together without sorrow. That is where warm and cold, light and dark begin; there fear commences. Read in the book whether it says anything about life; mankind thinks of nothing else, after all. Is it this for which we hear sighing, weeping and wailing? Why we call out, want, fear? Is this why the tears fall from your eyes? That will be it, for from afar I recall something about tears. It was dusk, there were trees, tears falling hence upon me. There were eyes all around and voices that sobbed. I think I was young then. But perhaps I remember because I long so, and no longer know yea or nay.

And again the tone of her voice rose to a high plaint:[2] Cold, cold, it is becoming colder than before. I knew it when I longed for this house.

And when he had wiped the tears she was no longer there. He heard stumbling and whispering on the stairs; he quickly opened the door and he saw the two maids going up slowly, pinafores held up to their faces. Reaching the window he drew the curtain aside. There was nothing to be seen outside but the lantern through the branches, a cloud, a star. And that it was cold, this he felt too, colder than at other times on such spring

[2] wail

evenings. He sat down again and pondered, but all that he thought was sorrow without end.

Next evening, at the window, he saw the thinnest crescent of the new moon floating in a vapour, its light already yellow however. When the young moon gleams clearly, he thought, fine weather is in the offing. He looked at the houses beyond the branches, all their doors closed and a lamp lit here and there. He noticed he was lonely, he sighed and drew the curtains. A servant knocked; she asked whether he had called, was there anything he wanted. Sir's so quiet, she said, it's upsetting us. No matter how softly you speak to yourself it can be heard downstairs. No, he said, your ears deceive you, I'm not talking with the books.

Silent, she lit the lamp and he went and sat down with the book and waited. The page turned over slowly.

And when the white woman was sitting there on the floor with her head raised up to him he looked straight into her eyes; there was something there deep down, something with a blue glow. About her face and hands there was something that moved.

Why cry and wait? she asked. After all, I have heard it ages ago, I have been driven here a long time. I know it because I wake up and notice how far the darkness is from the light, how much night differs from day. Of yesterday's event I know about sitting here and how much time has passed between then and now. Something has gone away, something has slipped down and I clearly remember that yesterday there were cries and I myself cried too. Today I have understood that there has been a moment, now past. And today it was full of rumours, many voices, many sobs, and weeping, more than I could hear. I don't know whether the waiting is here or there; I don't know whether it is I who waits or someone else. That is new and strange, the thought of another; it makes me soft, small, cold. It has hurt in my eyes and within me there is something: that tomorrow I shall know the great fear, darkness gaping open.

She laid down her head on the floor and wailed with a feeble sound, monotonously. Bending over her, he listened as his tears fell; he heard her softly asking each time: Why is it so dark? Why here? Why here? Why so dark?

He rose upright for he could not bear it; he covered his ears. But she had gone: there was only the crepuscular[3] light and the floor was empty.

There was a knock on the door; he went and saw the two servants, each with a tip of her pinafore in her hand. Did Sir call? asked the one and she trembled. Did Sir know how late the hour is? asked the other pleadingly; we're so afraid. He did not know what to say. But when they continued to stand there he said: Now just you go to bed.

The following evening rain was falling silently, the cobbles shone near the bridge, the sky was drab. Behind a window, beyond the lantern a reddish light gleamed. Past that house it was dark with trees and a dog began to howl there, high and long. Occasionally, when the howling grew fainter, it had the deep sound of a big dog, then it began afresh, helpless, intolerable. A figure, slowly mounting the bridge, halted and then descended into the dark of the trees. There was a sigh. He wondered why he stood here so often, watching, always in the direction of the bridge, watching the dark passage beneath the arch and its twin reflection on the canal water. The dog suddenly ceased howling; not a soul to be seen.

He drew the curtains, lit the lamp and took up the

[3] dim

book. While reading he looked round repeatedly but there was no one. And he read, page after page, until he noticed he had been sitting there a long time. He thought: Has it been a delusion of the senses? He thought even more, about this and other lives, about near and far, about now and tomorrow. And when he looked up she was sitting on the floor. She kept her white hands clenched tight together. Her voice sounded feeble and indistinct, tired, without hope: I do not know why I come here; I do not know where I must go and what I must think. I want to but I dare not. I have had peace here; it has been a moment and now another must come. Forget me; I shall forget you too.

Her head fell forwards; she sobbed noiselessly. And he did too, hands in front of his mouth.

Then he heard different sobs; he looked and saw the open book on the table, the floor without the whiteness that had been there. There was loud urgent knocking on the door; he answered hastily. The two maid-servants were standing there holding on to one another. Sir, Sir, oh merciful heavens, Sir! cried the one, and the other hid her face. But they touched him and became quiet. The one said: we heard Sir talking with something worse than we are capable of thinking. Quiet yourselves, he replied, go to bed and good night. They went up the stairs, slowly, dabbing their eyes.

He drew back the curtains and looked out into the night again. It was quiet. But beyond the bridge there was the small sound of a child just beginning to bawl. The branches moved in the wind. He mused as to what it was: something worse than one was capable of thinking; he mused whether truly he had seen anything at all.

The Elephant

by Slawomir Mrozek

The director of the Zoological Gardens had shown himself to be an upstart. He regarded his animals simply as stepping stones on the road of his own career. He was indifferent to the educational importance of his establishment. In his zoo the giraffe had a short neck, the badger had no burrow and the whistlers, having lost all interest, whistled rarely and with some reluctance. These shortcomings should not have been allowed, especially as the zoo was often visited by parties of schoolchildren.

The zoo was in a provincial town, and it was short of some of the most important animals, among them the elephant. Three thousand rabbits were a poor substitute for the noble giant. However, as our country developed, the gaps were being filled in a well-planned manner. On the occasion of the anniversary of the liberation,[1] on 22nd July, the zoo was notified that it had at long last been allocated an elephant. All the staff, who were devoted to their work, rejoiced at this news. All the greater was their surprise when they learned that the director had sent a letter to Warsaw, renouncing the allocation and putting forward a plan for obtaining an elephant by more economic means.

'I, and all the staff,' he had written, 'are fully aware how heavy a burden falls upon the shoulders of Polish

[1] liberation from German occupation in 1944

58

miners and foundry men because of the elephant. Desirous of reducing our costs, I suggest that the elephant mentioned in your communication should be replaced by one of our own procurement.[2] We can make an elephant out of rubber, of the correct size, fill it with air and place it behind railings. It will be carefully painted the correct colour and even on close inspection will be indistinguishable from the real animal. It is well known that the elephant is a sluggish animal and it does not run and jump about. In the notice on the railings we can state that this particular elephant is particularly sluggish. The money saved in this way can be turned to the purchase of a jet plane or the conservation of some church monument.

'Kindly note that both the idea and its execution are my modest contribution to the common task and struggle.

'I am, etc.'

This communication must have reached a soulless official, who regarded his duties in a purely bureaucratic manner and did not examine the heart of the matter but, following only the directive about reduction of expenditure, accepted the director's plan. On hearing the Ministry's approval, the director issued instructions for the making of the rubber elephant.

The carcass was to have been filled with air by two keepers blowing into it from opposite ends. To keep the operation secret the work was to be completed during the night because the people of the town, having heard that an elephant was joining the zoo, were anxious to see it. The director insisted on haste also because he expected a bonus, should his idea turn out to be a success.

[2] that we obtain ourselves

The two keepers locked themselves in a shed normally housing a workshop, and began to blow. After two hours of hard blowing they discovered that the rubber skin had risen only a few inches above the floor and its bulge in no way resembled an elephant. The night progressed. Outside, human voices were stilled and only the cry of the jackass interrupted the silence. Exhausted, the keepers stopped blowing and made sure that the air already inside the elephant should not escape. They were not young and were unaccustomed to this kind of work.

'If we go on at this rate,' said one of them, 'we shan't finish by morning. And what am I to tell my missus? She'll never believe me if I say that I spent the night blowing up an elephant.'

'Quite right,' agreed the second keeper. 'Blowing up an elephant is not an everyday job. And it's all because our director is a leftist.'

They resumed their blowing, but after another half-hour they felt too tired to continue. The bulge on the floor was larger but still nothing like the shape of an elephant.

'It's getting harder all the time,' said the first keeper.

'It's an uphill job, all right,' agreed the second. 'Let's have a little rest.'

While they were resting, one of them noticed a gas pipe ending in a valve. Could they not fill the elephant with gas? He suggested it to his mate.

They decided to try. They connected the elephant to the gas pipe, turned the valve, and to their joy in a few minutes there was a full-sized beast standing in the shed. It looked real: the enormous body, legs like columns, huge ears and the inevitable trunk. Driven by ambition the director had made sure of having in his zoo a very large elephant indeed.

'First class,' declared the keeper who had the idea of using gas. 'Now we can go home.'

In the morning the elephant was moved to a special run in a central position, next to the monkey cage. Placed in front of a large real rock it looked fierce and magnificent. A big notice proclaimed: 'Particularly sluggish. Hardly moves.'

Among the first visitors that morning was a party of children from the local school. The teacher in charge of them was planning to give them an object-lesson about the elephant. He halted the group in front of the animal and began:

'The elephant is a herbivorous mammal. By means of its trunk it pulls out young trees and eats their leaves.'

The children were looking at the elephant with enraptured admiration. They were waiting for it to pull out a young tree, but the beast stood still behind its railings.

'... The elephant is a direct descendant of the now-extinct mammoth. It's not surprising, therefore, that it's the largest living land animal.'

The more conscientious pupils were making notes.

'... Only the whale is heavier than the elephant, but then the whale lives in the sea. We can safely say that on land the elephant reigns supreme.'

A slight breeze moved the branches of the trees in the zoo.

'... The weight of a fully grown elephant is between nine and thirteen thousand pounds.'

At that moment the elephant shuddered and rose in the air. For a few seconds it swayed just above the ground, but a gust of wind blew it upward until its mighty silhouette was against the sky. For a short while people on the ground could see the four circles of its feet, its bulging belly and the trunk, but soon, propelled by the wind, the elephant sailed above the fence and disappeared above the treetops. Astonished monkeys in the cage continued staring into the sky.

They found the elephant in the neighbouring botanical gardens. It had landed on a cactus and punctured its rubber hide.

The schoolchildren who had witnessed the scene in the zoo soon started neglecting their studies and turned into hooligans. It is reported that they drink liquor and break windows. And they no longer believe in elephants.

Unexpected Guests

by Heinrich Böll

I have nothing against animals; on the contrary, I like them, and I enjoy caressing our dog's coat in the evening while the cat sits on my lap. It gives me pleasure to watch the children feeding the tortoise in the corner of the living-room. I have even grown fond of the baby hippopotamus we keep in our bathtub, and the rabbits running around loose in our apartment have long ceased to worry me. Besides, I am used to coming home in the evening and finding an unexpected visitor: a cheeping baby chick, or a stray dog my wife has taken in. For my wife is a good woman, she never turns anyone away from the door, neither man nor beast, and for many years now our children's evening prayers have wound up with the words: O Lord, please send us beggars and animals.

What is really worse is that my wife cannot say no to hawkers and peddlers, with the result that things accumulate in our home which I regard as superfluous – soap, razor-blades, brushes and darning wool – and lying around in drawers are documents which cause me some concern: an assortment of insurance policies and purchase agreements. My sons are insured for their education, my daughters for their trousseaux,[1] but we cannot feed them with either darning wool or soap

---

[1] traditionally a collection of clothing and linen reserved for a woman's marriage

until they get married or graduate, and it is only in exceptional cases that razor-blades are beneficial to the human system.

It will be readily understood, therefore, that now and again I show signs of slight impatience, although generally speaking I am known to be a quiet man. I often catch myself looking enviously at the rabbits who have made themselves at home under the table, munching away peacefully at their carrots, and the stupid gaze of the hippopotamus, who is hastening the accumulation of silt in our bathtub, causes me at times to stick out my tongue at him. And the tortoise stoically eating its way through lettuce leaves has not the slightest notion of the anxieties that swell my breast: the longing for some fresh, fragrant coffee, for tobacco, bread and eggs, and the comforting warmth engendered by a schnapps in the throats of careworn men. My sole comfort at such times is Billy, our dog, who, like me, is yawning with hunger. If, on top of all this, unexpected guests arrive – men unshaven like myself, or mothers with babies who get fed warm milk and moistened zwieback[2] – I have to get a grip on myself if I am to keep my temper. But I do keep it, because by this time it is practically the only thing I have left.

There are days when the mere sight of freshly boiled, snowy potatoes makes my mouth water; for – although I confess this reluctantly and with deep embarrassment – it is a long time since we have enjoyed 'good home cooking'. Our only meals are improvised ones of which we partake from time to time, standing up, surrounded by animals and human guests.

Fortunately it will be a while before my wife can buy useless articles again, for we have no more cash, my

[2] twice-baked bread, like a rusk

wages have been attached for an indefinite period, and I myself am reduced to spending the evenings going around the distant suburbs, in clothing that makes me unrecognisable, selling razor-blades, soap and buttons far below cost; for our situation has become grave. Nevertheless, we own several hundredweight of soap, thousands of razor-blades and buttons of every description, and towards midnight I stagger into the house and go through my pockets for money; my children, my animals, my wife stand around me with shining eyes, for I have usually bought some things on the way home: bread, apples, lard, coffee and potatoes – the latter, by the way, in great demand among the children as well as the animals – and during the nocturnal hours we gather together for a cheerful meal. Contented animals, contented children are all about me, my wife smiles at me, and we leave the living-room door open so the hippopotamus will not feel left out, his joyful grunts resounding from the bathroom. At that point my wife usually confesses to me that she has an extra guest hidden in the storeroom, who is only brought out when my nerves have been fortified by food: shy, unshaven men, rubbing their hands, take their place at table, women squeeze in between our children on the bench, milk is warmed up for crying babies. In this way I also make the acquaintance of animals that are new to me: seagulls, foxes and pigs, although once it was a small dromedary.[3]

'Isn't it cute?' asked my wife, and I was obliged to say yes, it was, while I anxiously watched the tireless munching of this duffel-coloured creature which looked at us out of slate-grey eyes. Fortunately the dromedary only stayed a week, and business was brisk: word had got

[3] camel

round of the quality of my merchandise, my reduced prices, and now and again I was even able to sell shoelaces and brushes, articles otherwise not much in demand. As a result, we experienced a period of false prosperity, and my wife, completely blind to the economic facts, produced a remark that worried me, 'Things are looking up!' But I saw our stocks of soap shrinking, the razor-blades dwindling, and even the supply of brushes and darning wool was no longer substantial.

Just about this time, when I could have used some spiritual sustenance, our house was shaken one evening, while we were all sitting peacefully together, by a tremor resembling a fair-sized earthquake: the pictures rattled, the table rocked, and a ring of fried sausage rolled off my plate. I was about to jump up and see what the matter was when I noticed suppressed laughter on the faces of my children. 'What's going on here?' I shouted, and for the first time in all my chequered experience I was really beside myself.

'Wilfred,' said my wife quietly, and put down her fork, 'it's only Wally.' She began to cry, and against her tears I have no defence, for she has borne me seven children.

'Who is Wally?' I asked wearily, and at that moment the house was rocked by another tremor. 'Wally,' said my youngest daughter, 'is the elephant we've got in the basement.'

I must admit I was at a loss, which is not really surprising. The largest animal we had housed so far had been the dromedary, and I considered an elephant too big for our apartment.

My wife and children, not in the least at a loss, supplied the facts: the animal had been brought to us for safekeeping by a bankrupt circus owner. Sliding down the chute which we otherwise use for our coal, it had had no trouble entering the basement. 'He rolled himself up into a ball,' said my eldest son, 'really an intelligent animal.' I did not doubt it, accepted the fact of Wally's presence, and was led down in triumph into the basement. The animal was not as large as all that; he waggled his ears and seemed quite at home with us, especially as he had a bale of hay at his disposal. 'Isn't he cute?' asked my wife, but I refused to agree. Cute did not seem to be the right word. Anyway, the family appeared disappointed at the limited extent of my enthusiasm, and my wife said, as we left the basement, 'How cruel you are, do you want him to be put up for auction?'

'What d'you mean, auction,' I said, 'and why cruel? Besides, it's against the law to conceal bankruptcy assets.'

'I don't care,' said my wife. 'Nothing must happen to the animal.'

In the middle of the night we were awakened by the circus owner, a diffident, dark-haired man, who asked us whether we had room for one more animal. 'It's my sole possession, all I have left in the world. Only for a night. How is the elephant, by the way?'

'He's fine,' said my wife, 'only I'm a bit worried about his bowels.'

'That'll soon settle down,' said the circus owner. 'It's just the new surroundings. Animals are so sensitive. How about it, then: will you take the cat too – just for the night?' He looked at me, and my wife nudged me and said, 'Don't be so unkind.'

'Unkind,' I said, 'no, I certainly don't want to be that. If you like, you can put the cat in the kitchen.'

'I've got it outside in the car,' said the man.

I left my wife to look after the cat and crawled back

into bed. My wife was a bit pale when she came to bed, and she seemed to be trembling.

'Are you cold?' I asked.

'Yes,' she said, 'I've got such funny chills.'

'You're just tired.'

'Maybe,' said my wife, but she gave me a queer look as she said it. We slept quietly, but in my dreams I still saw that queer look of my wife's, and a strange compulsion made me wake up earlier than usual. I decided to shave for once.

Lying under our kitchen table was a medium-sized lion; he was sleeping peacefully, only his tail moved gently and made a sound like someone playing with a very light ball.

I carefully lathered my face and tried not to make any noise, but when I turned my chin to the right to shave my left cheek I saw that the lion had his eyes open and was watching me. They really do look like cats, I thought. What the lion was thinking I don't know; he went on watching me, and I shaved, without cutting myself, but I must admit it is a strange feeling to shave with a lion looking on. My experience of handling wild beasts was practically nonexistent, so I confined myself to looking sternly at the lion, then I dried my face and went back to the bedroom. My wife was already awake, she was just about to say something, but I cut her short and exclaimed, 'What's the use of talking about it!' My wife began to cry, and I put my hand on her head and said, 'It's unusual, to say the least, you must admit that.'

'What isn't unusual?' said my wife, and I had no answer.

Meanwhile the rabbits had awakened, the children were making a racket in the bathroom, the hippopotamus – his name was Gottlieb – was already trumpeting away, Billy was stretching and yawning; only the tortoise was still asleep, but it sleeps most of the time anyway.

I let the rabbits into the kitchen, where their feed box is kept under the cupboard; the rabbits sniffed at the lion, the lion at the rabbits, and my children – uninhibited and used to animals as they are – were already in the kitchen. I almost had the feeling the lion was smiling; my third-youngest son immediately found a name for him: Bombilus. And Bombilus he remained.

A few days later someone came to take away the elephant and the lion. I must confess I saw the last of the elephant without regret; he seemed silly to me, while the lion's quiet, friendly dignity had endeared him to me. I felt a pang at Bombilus's departure. I had grown so used to him; he was really the first animal to enjoy my wholehearted affection.

'Oof,' he said.

by Quim Monzo

They drank coffee and ate pieces of almond cake. '*Oof,*' he said, eventually (because he had his mouth full before, not just of cake, but of lethargy, and he wouldn't have been able to open it). She didn't even look at him (it was *so* hot and the window, as usual ... shut ...). 'The window, as usual ... shut ...,' she said. He didn't answer (he thought it was only logical that it should be hot in the height of summer). 'Open it if you want,' he said, because he felt he ought to say something. But she didn't get up from her chair and she made no comment. The weather seemed to be silently crushing them. She picked up the teapot and slowly poured herself a cup of coffee (it was a year now since they'd broken the coffee pot, and they'd decided not to buy another one: as they didn't like tea, they could use the teapot for coffee). A fly was buzzing round the cake. She lifted her hand to frighten it, but decided the fly wasn't enough of a nuisance as to warrant the effort, so she let it be. The hand hung dreamily in the air for a moment. Then she lowered it slowly and left it on the table. 'I think,' he said, sniffing gently at the air, 'that this heat attracts the flies.' Outside the window, the sun was strangling the syphilitic[1] ivy that clung, more dead than alive, to the only clean patch of the dirty white wall. In no time at all the

[1] diseased

sunspot would get round to the window pane and would come into the room. 'Yes,' she agreed, turning her gaze on the cup and tapping it monotonously with the teaspoon (the ringing was constant and warm, minimal). 'Do you mind not making that noise?' he snapped. She let the teaspoon drop on to the table with a gentle, soft, orange-coloured sound. 'Before,' he went on talking, 'summer afternoons weren't so hot.' 'Everything's topsy-turvy,' they agreed. They sat in silence while the howl of the sun at its peak hung over everyone's head: those of the slow men in the street, of the children at the beach, blinded by the harshness. They shuffled the cards and cut the pack. She had a full house.

Before they realised, the sky was dark and the light black. They switched the light on and gathered up the cards. They turned the television on with the remote control. On the table there were still some sausage meats and pieces of cold toast, which they ate. Once all the programmes, anthems and flags were exhausted, the screen was flooded with rain and they fell asleep in the armchairs. Then, sometime around midnight, through the window came the pink she-doves and the black sugar-cane cockerels and the golden deer and the seagulls of lapis-lazuli and the ivory finches and the multi-coloured ivies and laughing heliotrope[2] giraffes. They stayed until dawn, and when the sun came up, they left slowly; so that when he and she woke up (the sun was already stabbing the white wall in front of the window), the animals and plants were gone. They drank coffee and ate pieces of almond cake. '*Oof*,' he said eventually (because he had his mouth full before and he wouldn't have been able to open it).

[2] growing towards the sun

71

Jennifer's Dreams

by Marie Luise Kaschnitz

On 2nd April Jennifer celebrated her eighth birthday. Her mother gave her a cake that she had baked herself and decorated with silver balls. She was allowed to invite her friends to tea. In the evening she spent an hour in her father's study. A lawyer by profession, her father's hobby was his tape-recorder and he spent his spare time recording and listening to tapes. That evening, to please Jennifer, Mr Andrew put on a symphony by Shostakovitch and stood up to conduct the orchestra. Jennifer looked at him in admiration believing that the notes really did sound at his command.

On 3rd April Jennifer described a dream to her mother when she woke up. She was walking over a hump-backed bridge. She saw a pond full of water lilies. Cows were standing up to their stomachs in the muddy water. A small red car was driven into the farmyard and the gravel crunched. Mrs Andrew was not particularly surprised and certainly not amused by all this, but Jennifer's face lit up and she laughed as she remembered her dream.

On 4th April Jennifer woke up with the same beaming expression as on the previous morning. She talked about cygnets and a room lined with mirrors where she wiped cobwebs from the misty glass. Mrs Andrew had to laugh at Jennifer's enthusiasm for it was a hard job getting the child to help with the housework in her waking hours.

On 5th April, having once heard that daytime experiences are relived in dreams, Mrs Andrew examined Jennifer's picture books and school books. But she found nothing that she could identify with her daughter's dreams. In the evening she told her husband about Jennifer's strange excitement whenever she talked about her dreams. She also mentioned that Jennifer never described her experiences as if they were dreams. She said, 'I was here and I was there, I did this and I did that.' None of this surprised Mr Andrew in the least.

On 7th April Jennifer woke up as cheerful as on all the previous days. But she said nothing, and Mrs Andrew began to ask her questions. 'Did you have another beautiful dream, doesn't my little mouse want to tell me anything at all today, come on, tell me.' Whereupon the excitement suddenly died in Jennifer's eyes and she chewed on her bread and jam with a sullen face.

On 8th April Mrs Andrew noticed that Jennifer looked pale and had rings round her eyes. She had her stool examined for worms, although she was convinced that Jennifer's sickly appearance was only due to her dreams.

By 10th April Jennifer was talking again and in a cheerful mood. 'I was in a garden with a hedge round it. I got lost but then I found my way. I rode a horse with a black mane. I was in a vault.' Mrs Andrew tried unsuccessfully to find out more about this 'vault'. But she heard only that Jennifer was not there alone, but with a woman, who dried her tears with a large handkerchief. 'You were crying then,' asked Mrs Andrew, surprised. Jennifer replied, 'Tears were running down my face, but not because I was unhappy.'

On the evening of 13th April Mrs Andrew grumbled

to her husband about Jennifer who would often fix her mother with a long, cold critical stare. 'Leave the child in peace,' said Mr Andrew, 'don't ask her any more questions, don't talk to her about it any more. This phase will pass too, perhaps quite soon.' Possibly precisely because of his serious and solitary nature, Mrs Andrew had great respect for her husband and she resolved not to ask Jennifer any more about her dreams. But she realised already that she would not abide by her resolution.

On 15th April Mrs Andrew went into town in the pouring rain to pick up a film that she had left to be developed. She had taken the pictures only recently. Several of them showed the little suburban house in the March sunshine; one of her husband in the garden digging the flower bed; one of Jennifer sitting on the front doorstep and staring into space in an indescribably disturbing manner. Mrs Andrew tore this last picture into small pieces and buried them in the dustbin under cabbage stalks and tea leaves.

On the morning of 17th April Jennifer talked again about the strange woman. The woman was washing rabbit meat in a dish and her hands were covered in blood. Jennifer was horrified and even wanted to run away. The woman did not scold her. She rinsed her hands thoroughly under running water and eventually there was no trace of blood left on them. The woman took Jennifer into the garden and put her arms around her. 'Did she kiss you too,' asked Mrs Andrew suspiciously. Jennifer did not say yes or no, but pulled a face as if the word kiss could not possibly describe the blissful nature of the contact. Mrs Andrew felt such a violent pang of jealousy that she did not dare admit it even to her husband.

On 21st April, having noticed that recently Jennifer

had wanted to go straight to bed after supper, rather than dawdling around endlessly as before, Mrs Andrew sat at her daughter's bedside for a full hour. She told stories about her childhood, read aloud and sang songs, the words of which she could not fully remember. 'How does it go on,' she asked, 'can you remember?' But Jennifer had stopped listening some time ago. She turned her face to the wall.

On 23rd April Mrs Andrew, who believed her daughter was bewitched, was toying with the idea of summoning one of those London priests who drive out evil spirits with all sorts of religious hocus-pocus. But she did not carry out her idea as it was not a case of disturbed sleep and also because she was afraid she would infuriate her husband with such superstitions.

On 25th April Mrs Andrew urged her daughter to tell her more about the strange woman. 'What does she look like, what's her hair like, how old is she, what clothes does she wear, do you sleep with her, and in what sort of room, what sort of bed?' Jennifer did not answer. She brought up her breakfast and could not leave for school for another hour.

On 30th April Jennifer brought up her breakfast again, although no one had mentioned her dreams this time. Mrs Andrew called the doctor who joked with Jennifer, made her say 'ah' and pulled back her eyelids. When Mrs Andrew saw that he couldn't think what else to do she impatiently sent him away. On the doorstep the doctor turned once more to Mrs Andrew and said, 'And what about you, Mrs Andrew?' and looked searchingly at her face. Mrs Andrew, who knew very well that she looked ill and jittery, said angrily, 'There's nothing wrong with me, I'm fine, I'm just worried about Jennifer, and I don't get any support from my husband, he doesn't bother about anything.'

On 3rd May Mrs Andrew was no longer sure that her husband had no wish to know about Jennifer's dreams, nor that he knew no more about them than she herself had told him. Towards evening, when she went into his room, Jennifer was sitting on a stool at his feet and he was playing with her long hair. It seemed to Mrs Andrew that the pair had been talking quietly to each other and were now silent like conspirators surprised in the act of making their plans. During the night Mrs Andrew sat up in bed sobbing and said, 'You and Jennifer, Jennifer and this woman, nobody cares about me, I'm quite alone.' Mr Andrew comforted her. He had never spoken to Jennifer about her dreams, she sometimes came into his room in the evening, mostly when he was playing music, but now and then for no particular reason.

On the morning of 10th May Jennifer talked to her mother again, more eagerly, but now it was only about the strange woman, her soft hands, her deep laugh, her fair hair. 'She is more beautiful than you. She is nicer than you.' And for the first time it occurred to Mrs Andrew that Jennifer was not dreaming at all, had never had these dreams, but was only inventing it all in order to hurt her. She tried to remember every detail of Jennifer's alleged stories. Wasn't there far too little that was irrational, didn't Jennifer continually meet the same woman in the same places? People don't dream like that, thought Mrs Andrew, that is how they make up stories, and for a particular purpose, an evil purpose no doubt.

On 13th May Mrs Andrew busied herself making the beds, shopping, cooking and ironing, but she could not shake off these thoughts. She was quite beside herself when she went to her husband before going to bed and said, 'I'm certain now that there haven't been any dreams, she's just a half-crazy, spiteful child.' Mr Andrew was alarmed. He pushed a chair towards his wife and smoothed her hair with his hand. Then he spoke soothingly to her again. They were all overwrought and needed to relax. He suggested a family trip, or rather, as the holidays were still a long way off, a weekend outing. The Andrews had no relatives and few friends who lived in the country. Finally Mrs Andrew remembered a couple who had once lived next door, but had moved to the country about nine years ago. The two young couples had become friendly in those days and they still exchanged New Year's greetings which always included a sincere invitation to visit. 'The Fergussons,' said Mrs Andrew, pleased that she had thought of them. Her husband agreed with her suggestion, if a little hesitantly.

On 16th May, a Thursday, the Andrews rang up their old friends Eddie and Liz. That day and the next were spent preparing for the outing. Jennifer packed her bits and pieces, acting quite her old self at the prospect of the short trip; she stayed up in the evening and sat with her parents as they traced the route on the map which would take them to their friends' isolated farm. Mrs Andrew made Jennifer a little kilt and finally they all washed the car together and were delighted to see it shining like new.

On 18th May as the Andrews set off at eight o'clock in the morning the weather was rather misty, nevertheless many flowers were in bloom in the suburban gardens, lilacs, viburnum and bleeding hearts. The small family had squashed up together on the front seats. Whenever the good-humoured father wanted to change gear, he said, 'Excuse me, ladies,' and Jennifer giggled and slid along a little. Mrs Andrew put her arm round her daughter. 'We should have done this long ago,' she thought. 'Once we get away from the daily routine, everything will be all right again.' At first Jennifer looked about her, her eyes shining, then she soon became sleepy and even fell asleep for a while. When she woke up at about eleven, the streets and houses had gone and there were fields and woods around her.

On 18th May at eleven o'clock the car had stopped at the side of the road. Mr and Mrs Andrew had spread the map out. They did not agree which road they should take at the next crossroads. 'Left,' said Jennifer calmly. The parents laughed, but then did turn left and drove on to a small village. At the end of the village they had another small difference of opinion at which Jennifer shook her head. 'Turn right,' she said, 'past the oak tree', and as a cyclist coming the other way gave the same advice, Mr Andrew turned right and drove past the oak tree. 'And where now, little clairvoyant?' he asked cheerfully, when the road forked again in the middle of a damp forest. After she had examined her surroundings in detail, Jennifer said, 'Now go left again down the sunken lane. When we're out of there, we'll be able to see the bridge.' Her face suddenly shone with happiness and she slid excitedly backwards and for-wards on her seat. 'Daddy can't drive like that,' said Mrs Andrew sharply, whilst her husband looked sideways at Jennifer in amazement. In the lane twigs hit the car windows. It smelt of snails and fungi. As they came out they saw a hump-backed bridge and a few stables. Cows stood up to their stomachs in a muddy pond. It was suddenly hot, almost oppressive, and Mrs Andrew pulled her silk scarf from her neck. 'We go up the hill to the house and round the stables,' said Jennifer, eagerly now. 'What would you know about it then, you know absolutely nothing,' said Mrs Andrew, who had suddenly lost her good humour. But it was correct. As they drove up the hill, the Andrews saw the house, rather a modest building, but given great distinction by some white magnolias. Liz Fergusson was standing on the steps and she now came running down across the yard. The Andrews were surprised to see how young she looked, almost younger than when they had known her in the past. 'And this is Jennifer,' said Mrs Andrew, after she had greeted her, and she turned round to the child. But the normally shy little girl had already put her arms round Liz Fergusson's neck and kissed her.

On 18th May at twelve o'clock the Andrews were walking around outside. They had not yet gone into the house with their old friend because they were still waiting for her husband. They saw a garden enclosed by a hedge, young swans and a colt with a black mane, and they stood on the same hump-backed bridge that they had driven over on their way. On the bridge Liz Fergusson bent down to Jennifer and said quietly, though loudly enough for Mrs Andrew to understand what she was saying, 'I don't have to explain anything to you, you know it all, you're always coming here', and Jennifer nodded happily. Next, they went through a crumbling underground passage. Jennifer was a little afraid in there and Liz grasped her shoulders and pulled her to her as if to protect her. Mrs Andrew was uneasy. She took her husband on one side and asked if they could drive back that evening. Mr Andrew had no objections, that would be fine by him.

On 18th May Eddie Fergusson drove into the yard in a red car. He was waving and shouting from a distance, and as soon as he got out, the happy neighbourly friendship started again from where it had left off. They had lunch in a kind of hall of mirrors and exchanged memories and cracked jokes over their meal and afterwards while they went for a walk and had their tea. Mrs Andrew was now in high spirits and she made an effort to ignore the fact that Jennifer had not let go of her old friend's hand and had not stopped gazing at her. She also chose not to notice a few glances between her husband and Liz Fergusson, although they were very strange looks; silent and deep and of an almost indecent intensity.

On 18th May at six o'clock the Andrews left, although they had been eagerly invited to stay the night many times. On the way home Jennifer slept against her father's chest, whilst Mrs Andrew drove. They did not talk, so as not to wake the child. When they reached home Mrs Andrew took Jennifer straight to bed. Then she did something she had not done for a long time; she went to see her husband in his study and listened while he played one of his tapes. The window was open and the air smelt of damp garden paths and new leaves. Mrs Andrew sat on the child's seat that Jennifer normally used. She looked bewildered and vacant as she had sometimes looked in her girlhood. 'We mustn't forget to ring for a plumber tomorrow,' she said, when the piano piece had ended. 'No, we mustn't,' said her husband, giving her a loving glance.

On 19th May, and from that day forward, Jennifer dawdled at bedtime and let her mother tell her one story after another. One morning she said, 'I had a dream,' and she related some nonsense. There was no more talk of the bridge, the cows in the water, the underground passage and the strange woman.

The Blue Jar

by Isak Dinesen

There was once an immensely rich old Englishman who
had been a courtier and a councillor to the Queen and
who now, in his old age, cared for nothing but collecting ancient blue china. To that end he travelled to
Persia, Japan and China, and he was everywhere accompanied by his daughter, the Lady Helena. It happened,
as they sailed in the Chinese Sea, that the ship caught
fire on a still night, and everybody went into the life-
boats and left her. In the dark and the confusion the
old peer was separated from his daughter. Lady Helena
got up on deck late, and found the ship quite deserted.
In the last moment a young English sailor carried her
down into a lifeboat that had been forgotten. To the
two fugitives it seemed as if fire was following them
from all sides, for the phosphorescence[1] played in the
dark sea, and, as they looked up, a falling star ran across
the sky, as if it was going to drop into the boat. They
sailed for nine days, till they were picked up by a Dutch
merchantman, and came home to England.

The old lord had believed his daughter to be dead.
He now wept with joy, and at once took her off to a
fashionable watering-place so that she might recover
from the hardships she had gone through. And as he
thought it must be unpleasant to her that a young
sailor, who made his bread in the merchant service,

[1] bright light

81

should tell the world that he had sailed for nine days alone with a peer's daughter, he paid the boy a fine sum, and made him promise to go shipping in the other hemisphere and never come back. 'For what,' said the old nobleman, 'would be the good of that?'

When Lady Helena recovered, and they gave her the news of the Court and of her family, and in the end also told her how the young sailor had been sent away never to come back, they found that her mind had suffered from her trials, and that she cared for nothing in all the world. She would not go back to her father's castle in its park, nor go to Court, nor travel to any gay town of the continent. The only thing which she now wanted to do was to go, like her father before her, to collect rare blue china. So she began to sail, from one country to the other, and her father went with her.

In her search she told the people, with whom she dealt, that she was looking for a particular blue colour, and would pay any price for it. But although she bought many hundred blue jars and bowls, she would always after a time put them aside and say: 'Alas, alas, it is not the right blue.' Her father, when they had sailed for many years, suggested to her that perhaps the colour which she sought did not exist. 'O God, Papa,' said she, 'how can you speak so wickedly? Surely there must be some of it left from the time when all the world was blue.'

Her two old aunts in England implored her to come back, still to make a great match. But she answered them: 'Nay, I have got to sail. For you must know, dear aunts, that it is all nonsense when learned people tell you that the seas have got a bottom to them. On the contrary, the water, which is the noblest of the elements, does, of course, go all through the earth, so that our planet really floats in the ether, like a soap bubble. And there, on the other hemisphere, a ship sails, with which I have got to keep pace. We two are like the reflection of one another, in the deep sea, and the ship of which I speak is always exactly beneath my own ship, upon the opposite side of the globe. You have never seen a big fish swimming underneath a boat, following it like a dark-blue shade in the water. But in that way this ship goes, like the shadow of my ship, and I draw it to and fro wherever I go , as the moon draws the tides, all through the bulk of the earth. If I stopped sailing, what would those poor sailors who made their bread in the merchant service do? But I shall tell you a secret,' she said. 'In the end my ship will go down, to the centre of the globe, and at the very same hour the other ship will sink as well – for people call it sinking, although I can assure you that there is no up and down in the sea – and there, in the midst of the world, we two shall meet.'

Many years passed, the old lord died and Lady Helena became old and deaf, but she still sailed. Then it happened, after the plunder of the summer palace of the Emperor of China, that a merchant brought her a very old blue jar. The moment she set eyes on it she gave a terrible shriek. 'There it is!' she cried. 'I have found it at last. This is the true blue. Oh, how light it makes one. Oh, it is as fresh as a breeze, as deep as a deep secret, as full as I say not what.' With trembling hands she held the jar to her bosom, and sat for six hours sunk in contemplation of it. Then she said to her doctor and her lady-companion: 'Now I can die. And when I am dead you will cut out my heart and lay it in the blue jar. For then everything will be as it was then. All shall be blue round me, and in the midst of the blue world my heart will be innocent and free, and will beat gently, like a wake that sings, like the drops that fall from an oar blade.' A little later she asked them: 'Is it not a sweet thing to think that, if only you have patience, all that has ever been will come back to you?' Shortly afterwards the old lady died.

Seven Floors

by Dino Buzzati

One morning in March, after a night's train journey, Giovanni Corte arrived in the town where the famous nursing home was. He was a little feverish, but he was still determined to walk from the station to the hospital, carrying his small bag.

Although his was an extremely slight case, in the very earliest stages, Giovanni Corte had been advised to go to the well-known sanatorium, which existed solely for the care of the particular illness from which he was suffering. This meant that the doctors were particularly competent and the equipment particularly pertinent and efficient.

Catching sight of it from a distance – he recognised it from having seen photos in some brochure – Giovanni Corte was most favourably impressed. The building was white, seven storeys high; its mass was broken up by a series of recesses which gave it a vague resemblance to a hotel. It was surrounded by tall trees.

After a brief visit from the doctor, prior to a more thorough one later on, Giovanni Corte was taken to a cheerful room on the seventh and top floor. The furniture was light and elegant, as was the wallpaper, there were wooden armchairs and brightly coloured cushions. The view was over one of the loveliest parts of the town. Everything was peaceful, welcoming and reassuring.

Giovanni Corte went to bed immediately, turned on

the reading-lamp at his bedside and began to read a book he had brought with him. After a few moments a nurse came in to see whether he needed anything.

He didn't, but was delighted to chat with the young woman and ask her questions about the nursing home. That was how he came to know its one extremely odd characteristic: the patients were housed on each floor according to the gravity of their state. The seventh, or top floor, was for extremely mild cases. The sixth was still for mild cases, but ones needing a certain amount of attention. On the fifth floor there were quite serious cases and so on, floor by floor. The second floor was for the very seriously ill. On the first floor were the hopeless cases.

This extraordinary system, apart from facilitating the general services considerably, meant that a patient only mildly affected would not be troubled by a dying co-sufferer next door and ensured a uniformity of atmosphere on each floor. Treatment, of course, would thus vary from floor to floor.

This meant that the patients were divided into seven successive castes. Each floor was a world apart, with its own particular rules and traditions. And as each floor was in the charge of a different doctor, slight but definite differences in the methods of treatment had grown up, although initially the director had given the institution a single basic bent.

As soon as the nurse had left the room Giovanni Corte, no longer feeling feverish, went to the window and looked out, not because he wanted to see the view of the town (although he was not familiar with it) but in the hopes of catching a glimpse, through the windows, of the patients on the lower floors. The structure of the building, with its large recesses, made this possible. Giovanni Corte concentrated particularly on the first

SEVEN FLOORS

floor windows, which looked a very long way away, and which he could see only obliquely. But he could see nothing interesting. Most of the windows were completely hidden by grey venetian blinds.

But Corte did see someone, a man, standing at a window right next to his own. The two looked at each other with a growing feeling of sympathy but did not know how to break the silence. At last Giovanni Corte plucked up courage and said: 'Have you just arrived too?'

'Oh no,' said his neighbour, 'I've been here two months.' He was silent for a few moments and then, apparently not sure how to continue the conversation, added: 'I was watching my brother down there.'

'Your brother?'

'Yes. We both came here at the same time, oddly enough, but he got worse – he's on the fourth now.'

'Fourth what?'

'Fourth floor,' explained the man, pronouncing the two words with such pity and horror that Giovanni Corte was vaguely alarmed.

'But in that case' – Corte proceeded with his questioning with the light-heartedness one might adopt when speaking of tragic matters which don't concern one – 'if things are already so serious on the fourth floor, whom do they put on the first?'

'Oh, the dying. There's nothing for the doctors to do down there. Only the priests. And of course . . . '

'But there aren't many people down there,' interrupted Giovanni Corte as if seeking confirmation, 'almost all the blinds are down.'

'There aren't many now, but there were this morning,' replied the other with a slight smile. 'The rooms with the blinds down are those where someone has died recently. As you can see, on the other floors

87

the shutters are all open. Will you excuse me,' he continued, moving slowly back in, 'it seems to be getting rather cold. I'm going back to bed. May I wish you all the best...'

The man vanished from the window sill and shut the window firmly; a light was lit inside the room. Giovanni Corte remained standing at the window, his eyes fixed on the lowered blinds of the first floor. He stared at them with morbid intensity, trying to visualise the ghastly secrets of that terrible first floor where patients were taken to die; he felt relieved that he was so far away. Meanwhile, the shadows of evening crept over the city. One by one the thousand windows of the sanatorium lit up, from the distance it looked like a great house lit up for a ball. Only on the first floor, at the foot of the precipice, did dozens of windows remain blank and empty.

Giovanni Corte was considerably reassured by the doctor's visit. A natural pessimist, he was already secretly prepared for an unfavourable verdict and wouldn't have been surprised if the doctor had sent him down to the next floor.

His temperature however showed no signs of going down, even though his condition was otherwise satisfactory. But the doctor was pleasant and encouraging. Certainly he was affected – the doctor said – but only very slightly; in two or three weeks he would probably be cured. 'So I'm to stay on the seventh floor?' inquired Giovanni Corte anxiously at this point.

'Well of course!' replied the doctor, clapping a friendly hand on his shoulder. 'Where did you think you were going? Down to the fourth perhaps?' He spoke jokingly, as though it were the most absurd thought in the world.

'I'm glad about that,' said Giovanni Corte. 'You know

how it is, when one's ill one always imagines the worst.' In fact he stayed in the room which he had originally been given. On the rare afternoons when he was allowed up he made the acquaintance of some of his fellow-patients. He followed the treatment scrupulously, concentrated his whole attention on making a rapid recovery, yet his condition seemed to remain unchanged.

About ten days later, the head nurse of the seventh floor came to see Giovanni Corte. He wanted to ask an entirely personal favour: the following day a woman with two children was coming to the hospital: there were two free rooms right next to his, but a third was needed; would Signor Corte mind very much moving into another, equally comfortable room?

Naturally, Giovanni Corte made no objection; he didn't mind what room he was in; indeed, he might have a new and prettier nurse.

'Thank you so much,' said the head nurse with a slight bow; 'though, mark you, such a courteous act doesn't surprise me coming from a person such as yourself. We'll start moving your things in about an hour, if you don't mind. By the way, it's one floor down,' he added in a quieter tone, as though it were a negligible detail. 'Unfortunately there are no free rooms on this floor. Of course it's a purely temporary arrangement,' he hastened to add, seeing that Corte had sat up suddenly and was about to protest, 'a purely temporary arrangement. You'll be coming up again as soon as there's a free room, which should be in two or three days.'

'I must confess,' said Giovanni Corte smiling, to show that he had no childish fears, 'I must confess that this particular sort of change of room doesn't appeal to me in the least.'

'But it has no medical basis; I quite understand what you mean, but in this case it's simply to do a favour for this woman who doesn't want to be separated from her children ... Now please,' he added, laughing openly, 'please don't get it into your head that there are other reasons!'

'Very well,' said Giovanni Corte, 'but it seems to me to bode ill.'

So Giovanni Corte went down to the sixth floor, and though he was convinced that this move did not correspond to any worsening in his own condition, he felt unhappy at the thought that there was now a definite barrier between himself and the everyday world of healthy people. The seventh floor was an embarkation point, with a certain degree of contact with society; it could be regarded as a sort of annexe to the ordinary world. But the sixth was already part of the real hospital; the attitudes of the doctors, nurses, of the patients themselves were just slightly different. It was admitted openly that the patients on that floor were really sick, even if not seriously so. From his initial conversation with his neighbours, staff and doctors, Giovanni Corte gathered that here the seventh floor was regarded as a joke, reserved for amateurs, all affectation and caprice;[1] it was only on the sixth floor that things began in earnest.

One thing Giovanni Corte did realise, however, was that he would certainly have some difficulty in getting back up to the floor where, medically speaking, he really belonged; to get back to the seventh floor he would have to set the whole complex organism of the place in motion, even for such a small move; it was quite plain that, were he not to insist, no one would

[1] pretence, and unpredictable changes of mood

ever have thought of putting him back on the top floor, with the 'almost-well'.

So Giovanni Corte decided not to forfeit anything that was his by right and not to yield to the temptations of habit. He was much concerned to impress upon his companions that he was with them only for a few days, that it was he who had agreed to go down a floor simply to oblige a lady, that he'd be going up again as soon as there was a free room. The others listened without interest and nodded, unconvinced.

Giovanni Corte's convictions, however, were confirmed by the judgement of the new doctor. He agreed that Giovanni Corte could most certainly be on the seventh floor; the form the disease had taken was ab-so-lute-ly negligible – he stressed each syllable so as to emphasise the importance of his diagnosis – but after all it might well be that Giovanni Corte would be better taken care of on the sixth floor.

'I don't want all that nonsense all over again,' Giovanni Corte interrupted firmly at this point, 'you say I should be on the seventh floor, and that's where I want to be.'

'No one denies that,' retorted the doctor. 'I was advising you not as a doc-tor, but as a re-al friend. As I say, you're very slightly affected, it wouldn't even be an exaggeration to say that you're not ill at all, but in my opinion what makes your case different from other similarly mild ones is its greater extension: the intensity of the disease is minimal, but it is fairly widespread; the destructive process of the cells' – it was the first time Giovanni Corte had heard the sinister expression – 'the destructive process of the cells is absolutely in the initial stage, it may not even have begun yet, but it is tending, I say tending, to affect large expanses of the organism. This is the only reason, in my opinion, why you might be better off down here on the sixth floor, where the methods of treatment are more highly specialised and more intensive.'

One day he was informed that the Director of the nursing home, after lengthy consultation with his colleagues, had decided to make a change in the subdivision of the patients. Each person's grade – so to speak – was to be lowered by half a point. From now on the patients on each floor were to be divided into two categories according to the seriousness of their condition (indeed the respective doctors had already made this subdivision, though exclusively for their own personal use) and the lower of these two halves was to be officially moved one floor down. For example half the patients on the sixth floor, those who were slightly more seriously affected, were to go down to the fifth; the less slightly affected of the seventh floor would go down to the sixth. Giovanni Corte was pleased to hear this, because his return to the seventh floor would certainly be much easier amid this highly complicated series of removals.

However, when he mentioned this hope to the nurse he was bitterly disappointed. He learned that he was indeed to be moved, not up to the seventh but down to the floor below. For reasons that the nurse was unable to explain, he had been classed among the more 'serious' patients on the sixth floor and so had to go down to the fifth.

Once he had recovered from his initial surprise, Giovanni Corte completely lost his temper; he shouted that they were cheating him, that he refused to hear of moving downwards, that he would go back home, that rights were rights and that the hospital administration could not afford to ignore the doctors' diagnosis so brazenly.

He was still shouting when the doctor arrived to explain matters more fully. He advised Corte to calm down unless he wanted his temperature to rise and explained that there had been a misunderstanding, at least in a sense. He agreed once again that Giovanni Corte would have been equally suitably placed on the seventh floor, but added that he had a slightly different, though entirely personal view of the case. Basically, in a certain sense, his condition could be considered as needing treatment on the sixth floor, because the symptoms were so widespread. But he himself failed to understand why Corte had been listed among the more serious cases of the sixth floor. In all probability the secretary, who had phoned him that very morning to ask about Giovanni Corte's exact medical position, had made a mistake in copying out his report. Or more likely still the administrative staff had purposely depreciated his own judgement, since he was considered an expert doctor but over optimistic. Finally, the doctor advised Corte not to worry, to accept the move without protest; what counted was the disease, not the floor on which the patient was placed.

As far as the treatment was concerned – added the doctor – Giovanni Corte would certainly not have cause for complaint: the doctor on the floor below was undoubtedly far more experienced; it was almost part of the system that the doctors became more experienced, at least in the eyes of the administration, the further down you went. The rooms were equally comfortable and elegant. The view was equally good; it was only from the third floor that it was cut off by the surrounding trees.

It was evening, and Giovanni Corte's temperature had risen accordingly; he listened to this meticulous ratiocination with an increasing feeling of exhaustion.

Finally he realised that he had neither the strength nor the desire to resist this unfair removal any further. Unprotesting, he allowed himself to be taken one floor down.

Giovanni Corte's one meagre consolation on the fifth floor was the knowledge that, in the opinion of doctors, nurses and patients alike, he was the least seriously ill of anyone on the whole floor. In short, he could consider himself much the most fortunate person in that section. On the other hand he was haunted by the thought that there were now two serious barriers between himself and the world of ordinary people.

As spring progressed the weather became milder, but Giovanni Corte no longer liked to stand at the window as he used to do; although it was stupid to feel afraid, he felt a strange movement of terror at the sight of the first floor windows, always mostly closed and now so much nearer.

His own state seemed unchanged; though after three days on the fifth floor a patch of eczema appeared on his right leg and showed no signs of clearing up during the following days. The doctor assured him that this was something absolutely independent of the main disease; it could have happened to the most healthy person in the world. Intensive treatment with digamma rays would clear it up in a few days.

'And can't one have that here?' asked Giovanni Corte.

'Certainly', replied the doctor delighted; 'we have everything here. There's only one slight inconvenience...'

'What?' asked Giovanni Corte with vague foreboding.

'Inconvenience in a manner of speaking,' the doctor corrected himself. 'The fourth floor is the only one with the relevant apparatus and I wouldn't advise you to go up and down three times a day.'

'So it's out of the question?'

'It would really be better if you would be good enough to go down to the fourth floor until the eczema has cleared up.'

'That's enough,' shrieked Giovanni Corte exasperated. 'I've had enough of going down! I'd rather die than go down to the fourth floor!'

'As you wish,' said the doctor soothingly, so as not to annoy him, 'but as the doctor responsible, I must point out that I forbid you to go up and down three times a day.'

The unfortunate thing was that the eczema, rather than clearing up, began to spread gradually. Giovanni Corte couldn't rest, he tossed and turned in bed. His anger held out for three days but finally he gave in. Of his own accord, he asked the doctor to arrange for the ray treatment to be carried out, and to move to the floor below.

Here Corte noticed, with private delight, that he really was an exception. The other patients on the floor were certainly much more seriously affected and unable to move from their beds at all. He, on the other hand, could afford the luxury of walking from his bedroom to the room where the rays were, amid the compliments and amazement of the nurses themselves.

He made a point of stressing the extremely special nature of his position to the new doctor. A patient who, basically, should have been on the seventh floor was in fact on the fourth. As soon as his eczema was better, he would be going up again. This time there could be absolutely no excuse. He, who could still legitimately have been on the seventh floor!

'On the seventh?' exclaimed the doctor who had just

finished examining him, with a smile. 'You sick people do exaggerate so! I'd be the first to agree that you should be pleased with your condition; from what I see from your medical chart, it hasn't changed much for the worse. But – forgive my rather brutal honesty – there's quite a difference between that and the seventh floor. You're one of the least worrying cases, I quite agree, but you're definitely ill.'

'Well then,' said Giovanni Corte, scarlet in the face, 'what floor would you personally put me on?'

'Well really, it's not easy to say, I've only examined you briefly, for any final judgement I'd have to observe you for at least a week.'

'All right,' insisted Corte, 'but you must have some idea.'

To calm him, the doctor pretended to concentrate on the matter for a moment and then, nodding to himself, said slowly: 'Oh dear! Look, to please you, I think after all one might say the sixth. Yes,' he added as if to persuade himself of the rightness of what he was saying, 'the sixth would probably be all right.'

The doctor thought that this would please his patient. But an expression of terror spread over Giovanni Corte's face: he realised that the doctors of the upper floors had deceived him; here was this new doctor, plainly more expert and honest, who in his heart of hearts – it was quite obvious – would place him not on the seventh but on the sixth floor, possibly even the lower fifth! The unexpected disappointment prostrated Corte. That evening his temperature rose appreciably.

His stay on the fourth floor was the most peaceful period he had had since coming to the hospital. The doctor was a delightful person, attentive and pleasant; he often stayed for whole hours to talk about all kinds of things. Giovanni Corte too was delighted to have an opportunity to talk, and drew the conversation around to his normal past life as a lawyer and man of the world. He tried to convince himself that he still belonged to the society of healthy men, that he was still connected with the world of business, that he was really still interested in matters of public import. He tried, but unsuccessfully. The conversation invariably came round, in the end, to the subject of his illness.

The desire for any sign of improvement had become an obsession. Unfortunately the digamma rays had succeeded in preventing the spread of the eczema but they had not cured it altogether. Giovanni Corte talked about this at length with the doctor every day and tried to appear philosophical, even ironic about it, without ever succeeding.

'Tell me, doctor,' he said one day, 'how is the destructive process of the cells coming along?'

'What a frightful expression,' said the doctor reprovingly. 'Wherever did you come across that? That's not at all right, particularly for a patient. I never want to hear anything like that again.'

'All right,' objected Corte, 'but you still haven't answered.'

'I'll answer right away,' replied the doctor pleasantly. 'The destructive process of your cells, to use your own horrible expression is, in your very minor case, absolutely negligible. But obstinate, I must say.'

'Obstinate, you mean chronic?'

'Now don't credit me with things I haven't said. I only said obstinate. Anyhow that's how it is in minor cases. Even the mildest infections often need long and intensive treatment.'

'But tell me, doctor, when can I expect to see some improvement?'

97

'When? It's difficult to say in these cases... But listen,' he added after pausing for thought, 'I can see that you're positively obsessed with the idea of recovery... if I weren't afraid of angering you, do you know what I'd suggest?'

'Please do say...'

'Well, I'll put the situation very clearly. If I had this disease even slightly and were to come to this sanatorium, which is probably the best there is, I would arrange of my own accord, and from the first day – I repeat from the first day – to go down to one of the lower floors. In fact I'd even go to the...'

'To the first?' suggested Corte with a forced smile.

'Oh dear no!' replied the doctor with a deprecating smile, 'Oh dear no! But to the third or even the second. On the lower floors the treatment is far better, you know, the equipment is more complete, more powerful, the staff are more expert. And then you know who is the real soul of this hospital?'

'Isn't it Professor Dati?'

'Exactly. It was he who invented the treatment carried out here, he really planned the whole place. Well, Dati, the master-mind, operates, so to speak, between the first and second floors. His driving force radiates from there. But I assure you that it never goes beyond the third floor: further up than that the details of his orders are glossed over, interpreted more slackly; the heart of the hospital is on the lowest floors, and that's where you must be to have the best treatment.'

'So in short,' said Giovanni Corte, his voice shaking, 'so you would advise me...'

'And there's something else,' continued the doctor unperturbed, 'and that is that in your case there's also the eczema to be considered. I agree that it's quite unimportant, but it is rather irritating, and in the long run it might lower your morale; and you know how important peace of mind is for your recovery. The rays have been only half successful. Now why? It might have been pure chance, but it might also have been that they weren't sufficiently intense. Well, on the third floor the apparatus is far more powerful. The chances of curing your eczema would be much greater. And the point is that once the cure is under way, the hardest part is over. Once you really feel better, there's absolutely no reason why you shouldn't come up here again, or indeed higher still, according to your "deserts", to the fifth, the sixth, possibly even the seventh . . . '

'But do you think this will hasten my recovery?'

'I've not got the slightest doubt it will. I've already said what I'd do if I were in your place.'

The doctor talked like this to Giovanni Corte every day. And at last, tired of the inconveniences of the eczema, despite his instinctive reluctance to go down a floor, he decided to take the doctor's advice and move to the floor below.

He noticed immediately that the third floor was possessed of a special gaiety affecting both doctors and nurses, even though the cases treated on that floor were very serious. He noticed too that this gaiety increased daily; consumed with curiosity, as soon as he got to know the nurse, he asked why on earth they were all so cheerful.

'Oh, didn't you know?' she replied, 'in three days' time we're all going on holiday.'

'On holiday?'

'That's right. The whole floor closes for a fortnight and the staff go off and enjoy themselves. Each floor takes it in turns to have a holiday.'

'And what about the patients?'

'There are relatively few of them, so two floors are converted into one.'

'You mean you put the patients of the third and fourth floors together?'

'No, no,' the nurse corrected him, 'of course the third and second. The patients on this floor will have to go down.'

'Down to the second?' asked Giovanni Corte, suddenly pale as death. 'You mean I'll have to go down to the second?'

'Well, yes. What's so odd about that? When we come back, in a fortnight, you'll come back here, in this same room. I can't see anything so terrifying about it.'

But Giovanni Corte – as if forewarned by some strange instinct – was horribly afraid. However, since he could hardly prevent the staff from going on their holidays, and convinced that the new treatment with the stronger rays would do him good – the eczema had almost cleared up – he didn't dare offer any formal opposition to this new move. But he did insist, despite nurses' banter, that the label on the door of his new room should read 'Giovanni Corte, third floor, temporary'. Such a thing had never been done before in the whole history of the sanatorium, but the doctors didn't object, fearing that the prohibition of even such a minor matter might cause a serious shock to a patient as highly strung as Giovanni Corte.

After all, it was simply a question of waiting for fourteen days, neither more nor less. Giovanni Corte began to count them with stubborn eagerness, lying motionless on his bed for hours on end, staring at the furniture, which wasn't as pleasant and modern here as on the higher floors, but more cumbersome, gloomy and severe. Every now and again he would listen intently, thinking he heard sounds from the floor below, the floor of the dying, the 'condemned' – vague sounds of death in action.

Naturally he found all this very dispiriting. His agitation seemed to nourish the disease, his temperature began to rise, the state of continued weakness began to affect him vitally. From the window – which was almost always open, since it was now mid-summer – he could no longer see the roofs nor even the houses, but only the green wall of the surrounding trees.

A week later, one afternoon about two o'clock, his room was suddenly invaded by the head nurse and three nurses, with a trolley. 'All ready for the move, then?' asked the head nurse jovially.

'What move?' asked Giovanni Corte weakly, 'what's all this? The third floor staff haven't come back after a week have they?'

'Third floor?' repeated the head nurse uncomprehendingly, 'my orders are to take you down to the first floor,' and he produced a printed form for removal to the first floor signed by none other than Professor Dati himself.

Giovanni Corte gave vent to his terror, his diabolical rage in long angry shrieks, which resounded throughout the whole floor. 'Less noise, please,' begged the nurses, 'there are some patients here who are not at all well.' But it would have taken more than that to calm him.

At last the second-floor doctor appeared – a most attentive person. After being given the relevant information he looked at the form and listened to Giovanni Corte's side of the story. He then turned angrily to the head nurse and told him there had been a mistake, he himself had had no such orders, for some time now the place had been an impossible muddle, he himself knew nothing about what was going on . . . At last, when he

101

had had his say with his inferior, he turned politely to his patient, highly apologetic.

'Unfortunately, however,' he added, 'unfortunately Professor Dati left the hospital about an hour ago – he'll be away for a couple of days. I'm most awfully sorry, but his orders can't be overlooked. He would be the first to regret it, I assure you . . . an absurd mistake! I fail to understand how it could have happened!'

Giovanni Corte had begun to tremble piteously. He was now completely unable to control himself, overcome with fear like a small child. His slow desperate sobbing echoed throughout the room.

It was as a result of this execrable mistake, then, that he was removed to his last resting place: he who basically, according to the most stringent medical opinion, was fit for the sixth, if not the seventh floor as far as his illness was concerned! The situation was so grotesque that from time to time Giovanni Corte felt inclined simply to roar with laughter.

Stretched out on his bed, while the afternoon warmth flowed calmly over the city, he would stare at the green of the trees through the window and feel that he had come to a completely unreal world, walled in with sterilised tiles, full of deathly arctic passages and soulless white figures. It even occurred to him that the trees he thought he saw through the window were not real; finally, when he noticed that the leaves never moved, he was certain of it.

Corte was so upset by this idea that he called the nurse and asked for his spectacles, which he didn't use in bed, being short-sighted; only then was he a little reassured: the lenses proved that they were real leaves and that they were shaken, though very slightly, by the wind.

When the nurse had gone out, he spent half an hour

in complete silence. Six floors, six solid barriers, even if only because of a bureaucratic mistake, weighed implacably above Giovanni Corte. How many years (for obviously it was now a question of years) would it be before he could climb back to the top of that precipice?

But why was the room suddenly going so dark? It was still mid-afternoon. With a supreme effort, for he felt himself paralysed by a strange lethargy, Giovanni Corte turned to look at his watch on the locker by his bed. Three-thirty. He turned his head the other way and saw that the venetian blinds, in obedience to some mysterious command, were dropping slowly, shutting out the light.

The Bound Man

by Ilse Aichinger

Sunlight on his face woke him, but made him shut his eyes again; it streamed unhindered down the slope, collected itself into rivulets, attracted swarms of flies, which flew low over his forehead, circled, sought to land, and were overtaken by fresh swarms. When he tried to whisk them away he discovered that he was bound. A thin rope cut into his arms. He dropped them, opened his eyes again, and looked down at himself. His legs were tied all the way up to his thighs; a single length of rope was tied round his ankles, crisscrossed all the way up his legs, and encircled his hips, his chest and his arms. He could not see where it was knotted. He showed no sign of fear or hurry, though he thought he was unable to move, until he discovered that the rope allowed his legs some free play, and that round his body it was almost loose. His arms were tied to each other but not to his body, and had some free play too. This made him smile, and it occurred to him that perhaps children had been playing a practical joke on him.

He tried to feel for his knife, but again the rope cut softly into his flesh. He tried again, more cautiously this time, but his pocket was empty. Not only his knife, but the little money that he had on him, as well as his coat, were missing. His shoes had been pulled from his feet and taken too. When he moistened his lips he tasted blood, which had flowed from his temples down his cheeks, his chin, his neck, and under his shirt. His eyes were painful; if he kept them open for long he saw reddish stripes in the sky.

He decided to stand up. He drew his knees up as far as he could, rested his hands on the fresh grass and jerked himself to his feet. An elder-branch stroked his cheek, the sun dazzled him, and the rope cut into his flesh. He collapsed to the ground again, half out of his mind with pain, and then tried again. He went on trying until the blood started flowing from his hidden weals. Then he lay still again for a long while, and let the sun and the flies do what they liked.

When he awoke for the second time the elder-bush had cast its shadow over him, and the coolness stored in it was pouring from between its branches. He must have been hit on the head. Then they must have laid him down carefully, just as a mother lays her baby behind a bush when she goes to work in the fields.

His chances all lay in the amount of free play allowed him by the rope. He dug his elbows into the ground and tested it. As soon as the rope tautened he stopped, and tried again more cautiously. If he had been able to reach the branch over his head he could have used it to drag himself to his feet, but he could not reach it. He laid his head back on the grass, rolled over, and struggled to his knees. He tested the ground with his toes, and then managed to stand up almost without effort.

A few paces away lay the path across the plateau, and among the grass were wild pinks and thistles in bloom. He tried to lift his foot to avoid trampling on them, but the rope round his ankles prevented him. He looked down at himself.

The rope was knotted at his ankles, and ran round his legs in a kind of playful pattern. He carefully bent and tried to loosen it, but, loose though it seemed to be, he could not make it any looser. To avoid treading on the thistles with his bare feet he hopped over them like a bird.

The cracking of a twig made him stop. People in this district were very prone to laughter. He was alarmed by the thought that he was in no position to defend himself. He hopped on until he reached the path. Bright fields stretched far below. He could see no sign of the nearest village, and, if he could move no faster than this, night would fall before he reached it.

He tried walking, and discovered that he could put one foot before another if he lifted each foot a definite distance from the ground and then put it down again before the rope tautened. In the same way he could actually swing his arms a little.

After the first step he fell. He fell right across the path, and made the dust fly. He expected this to be a sign for the long-suppressed laughter to break out, but all remained quiet. He was alone. As soon as the dust had settled he got up and went on. He looked down and watched the rope slacken, grow taut, and then slacken again.

When the first glow-worms appeared he managed to look up. He felt in control of himself again, and his impatience to reach the nearest village faded.

Hunger made him light-headed, and he seemed to be going so fast that not even a motor-cycle could have overtaken him; alternatively he felt as if he were standing still and that the earth was rushing past him, like a river flowing past a man swimming against the stream. The stream carried branches which had been bent southwards by the north wind, stunted young trees, and patches of grass with bright, long-stalked flowers. It ended by submerging the bushes and the young trees, leaving only the sky and the man above water-level. The moon had risen, and illuminated the bare, curved summit of the plateau, the path, which was overgrown with young grass, the bound man making his way along it with quick, measured steps, and two hares, which ran across the hill just in front of him and vanished down the slope. Though the nights were still cool at this time of the year, before midnight the bound man lay down at the edge of the escarpment and went to sleep.

In the light of morning the animal-tamer who was camping with his circus in the field outside the village saw the bound man coming down the path, gazing thoughtfully at the ground. The bound man stopped and bent down. He held out one arm to help keep his balance and with the other picked up an empty wine-bottle. Then he straightened himself and stood erect again. He moved slowly, to avoid being cut by the rope, but to the circus proprietor what he did suggested the voluntary limitation of an enormous swiftness of movement. He was enchanted by its extraordinary gracefulness, and while the bound man looked about for a stone on which to break the bottle, so that he could use the splintered neck to cut the rope, the animal-tamer walked across the field and approached him. The first leaps of a young panther had never filled him with such delight.

'Ladies and gentlemen, the bound man!' His very first movements let loose a storm of applause, which out of sheer excitement caused the blood to rush to the cheeks of the animal-tamer standing at the edge of the arena. The bound man rose to his feet. His surprise whenever he did this was like that of a four-footed animal which has managed to stand on its hind-legs. He knelt, stood up, jumped, and turned cart-wheels. The spectators found it as astonishing as if they had seen a bird which voluntarily remained earthbound, and confined itself to hopping. The bound man became an enormous draw. His absurd steps and little jumps, his elementary exercises in movement, made the rope-dancer superfluous. His fame grew from village to village, but the motions he went through were few and always the same, they were really quite ordinary motions, which he had continually to practise in the daytime in the half-dark tent in order to retain his shackled freedom. In that he remained entirely within the limits set by his rope he was free of it, it did not confine him, but gave him wings and endowed his leaps and jumps with purpose; just as the flights of birds of passage have purpose when they take wing in the warmth of summer and hesitantly make small circles in the sky.

All the children of the neighbourhood started playing games of 'bound man'. They formed rival gangs, and one day the circus people found a little girl lying bound in a ditch, with a cord tied round her neck so that she could hardly breathe. They released her, and at the end of the performance that night the bound man made a speech. He announced briefly that there was no sense in being tied up in such a way that you could not jump. After that he was regarded as a comedian.

Grass and sunlight, tent-pegs driven into the ground and then pulled up again, and on to the next village. 'Ladies and gentlemen, the bound man!' The summer mounted towards its climax. It bent its face deeper over the fish-ponds in the hollows, taking delight in its dark reflection, skimmed the surface of the rivers, and made the plain into what it was. Everyone who could walk went to see the bound man.

Many wanted a close-up view of how he was bound. So the circus proprietor announced after each performance that anyone who wanted to satisfy himself that the knots were real and the rope not made of rubber was at liberty to do so. The bound man generally waited for the crowd in the area outside the tent. He laughed or remained serious, and held out his arms for inspection. Many took the opportunity to look him in the face, others gravely tested the rope, tried the knots on his ankles, and wanted to know exactly how the lengths compared with the length of his limbs. They asked him how he had come to be tied up like that, and he answered patiently, always saying the same thing. Yes, he had been tied up, he said, and when he awoke he found that he had been robbed as well. Those who had done it must have been pressed for time, because they had tied him up somewhat too loosely for someone who was not supposed to be able to move and somewhat too tightly for someone who was expected to be able to move. But he did move, people pointed out. Yes, he replied, what else could he do?

Before he went to bed he always sat for a time in front of the fire. When the circus proprietor asked him why he didn't make up a better story, he always answered that he hadn't made up that one, and blushed. He preferred staying in the shade.

The difference between him and the other performers was that when the show was over he did not take off his rope. The result was that every movement that he made was worth seeing, and the villagers used to hang about the camp for hours, just for the sake of seeing him get up from in front of the fire and roll himself in his blanket. Sometimes the sky was beginning to lighten when he saw their shadows disappear.

The circus proprietor often remarked that there was no reason why he should not be untied after the evening performance and tied up again next day. He pointed out that the rope-dancers, for instance, did not stay on their rope over night. But no one took the idea of untying him seriously.

For the bound man's fame rested on the fact that he was always bound, that whenever he washed himself he had to wash his clothes too and *vice versa*, and that his only way of doing so was to jump in the river just as he was every morning when the sun came out, and that he had to be careful not to go too far out for fear of being carried away by the stream.

The proprietor was well aware that what in the last resort protected the bound man from the jealousy of the other performers was his helplessness; he deliberately left them the pleasure of watching him groping painfully from stone to stone on the river bank every morning with his wet clothes clinging to him. When his wife pointed out that even the best clothes would not stand up indefinitely to such treatment (and the bound man's clothes were by no means of the best) he replied curtly that it was not going to last for ever. That was his answer to all objections – it was for the summer season only. But when he said this he was not being serious; he was talking like a gambler who has no intention of giving up his vice. In reality he would have been prepared cheerfully to sacrifice his lions and his rope-dancers for the bound man.

He proved this on the night when the rope-dancers jumped over the fire. Afterwards he was convinced that they did it, not because it was midsummer's day, but because of the bound man, who as usual was lying and watching them, with that peculiar smile that might have been real or might have been only the effect of the glow on his face. In any case no one knew anything about him, because he never talked about anything that had happened to him before he emerged from the wood that day.

But that evening two of the performers suddenly picked him up by the arms and legs, carried him to the edge of the fire and started playfully swinging him to and fro, while two others held out their arms to catch him on the other side. In the end they threw him, but too short. The two men on the other side drew back – they explained afterwards that they did so the better to take the shock. The result was that the bound man landed at the very edge of the flames and would have been burned if the circus proprietor had not seized his arms and quickly dragged him away to save the rope which was starting to get singed. He was certain that the object had been to burn the rope. He sacked the four men on the spot.

A few nights later the proprietor's wife was awakened by the sound of footsteps on the grass, and went outside just in time to prevent the clown from playing his last practical joke. He was carrying a pair of scissors. When he was asked for an explanation he insisted that he had had no intention of taking the bound man's life, but only wanted to cut his rope, because he felt sorry for him. But he was sacked too.

These antics amused the bound man, because he could have freed himself if he had wanted to whenever he liked, but perhaps he wanted to learn a few new jumps first. The children's rhyme: 'We travel with the circus, we travel with the circus' sometimes occurred to him while he lay awake at night. He could hear the voices of spectators on the opposite bank who had been driven too far downstream on the way home. He could see the river gleaming in the moonlight, and the young shoots growing out of the thick tops of the willow trees, and did not think about autumn yet.

The circus proprietor dreaded the danger involved for the bound man by sleep. Attempts were continually made to release him while he slept. The chief culprits were sacked rope-dancers, or children who were bribed for the purpose. But measures could be taken to safeguard against these. A much bigger danger was that which he represented to himself. In his dreams he forgot his rope, and was surprised by it when he woke in the darkness of morning. He would angrily try to get up, but lose his balance and fall back again. The previous evening's applause was forgotten, sleep was still too near, his head and neck too free. He was just the opposite of a hanged man – his neck was the only part of him that was free. You had to make sure that at such moments no knife was within his reach. In the early hours of the morning the circus proprietor sometimes sent his wife to see whether the bound man was all right. If he was asleep she would bend over him and feel the rope. It had grown hard from dirt and damp. She would test the amount of free play it allowed him, and touch his tender wrists and ankles.

The most varied rumours circulated about the bound man. Some said he had tied himself up and invented the story of having been robbed, and towards the end of the summer that was the general opinion. Others maintained that he had been tied up at his own request, perhaps in league with the circus proprietor. The hesitant way in which he told his story, his habit of breaking off when the talk got round to the attack on him, contributed greatly to these rumours. Those who still believed in the robbery-with-violence story were laughed at. Nobody knew what difficulties the circus proprietor had in keeping the bound man, and how often he said he had had enough and wanted to clear off, for too much of the summer had passed.

Later, however, he stopped talking about clearing off. When the proprietor's wife brought him his food by the river and asked him how long he proposed to remain with them, he did not answer. She thought he had got used, not to being tied up, but to not forgetting for a moment that he was tied up – the only thing that anyone in his position could get used to. She asked him whether he did not think it ridiculous to be tied up all the time, but he answered that he did not. Such a variety of people – clowns, freaks, and comics, to say nothing of elephants and tigers – travelled with circuses that he did not see why a bound man should not travel with a circus too. He told her about the movements he was practising, the new ones he had discovered, and about a new trick that had occurred to him while he was whisking flies from the animals' eyes. He described to her how he always anticipated the effect of the rope and always restrained his movements in such a way as to prevent it from ever tautening; and she knew that there were days when he was hardly aware of the rope when he jumped down from the wagon and slapped the flanks of the horses in the morning, as if he were moving in a dream. She watched him vault over the bars almost without touching them, and saw the sun on his face, and he told her that sometimes he felt as if he were not tied up at all. She answered that if he were prepared to be untied there would never be any need for him to feel tied up. He agreed that he could be untied whenever he felt like it.

The woman ended by not knowing whether she were more concerned with the man or with the rope that tied him. She told him that he could go on travelling with the circus without his rope, but she did not believe it. For what would be the point of his antics without his rope, and what would he amount to without it? Without his rope he would leave them, and the happy days would be over. She would no longer be able to sit beside him on the stones by the river without rousing suspicion, and she knew that his continued presence, and her conversations with him, of which the rope was the only subject, depended on it. Whenever she agreed that the rope had its advantages he would start talking about how troublesome it was, and whenever he started talking about its advantages she would urge him to get rid of it. All this seemed as endless as the summer itself.

At other times she was worried at the thought that she was herself hastening the end by her talk. Sometimes she would get up in the middle of the night and run across the grass to where he slept. She wanted to shake him, wake him up and ask him to keep the rope. But then she would see him lying there; he had thrown off his blanket, and there he lay like a corpse, with his legs outstretched and his arms close together, with the rope tied round them. His clothes had suffered from the heat and the water, but the rope had grown no thinner. She felt that he would go on travelling with the circus until the flesh fell from him and exposed the joints. Next morning she would plead with him more ardently than ever to get rid of his rope.

The increasing coolness of the weather gave her hope. Autumn was coming, and he would not be able to go on jumping into the river with his clothes on much longer. But the thought of losing his rope, about which he had felt indifferent earlier in the season, now depressed him.

The songs of the harvesters filled him with foreboding. 'Summer has gone, summer has gone.' But he realised that soon he would have to change his clothes, and he was certain that when he had been untied it would be impossible to tie him up again in exactly the same way. About this time the proprietor started talking about travelling south that year.

The heat changed without transition into quiet, dry cold, and the fire was kept in all day long. When the bound man jumped down from the wagon he felt the coldness of the grass under his feet. The stalks were bent with ripeness. The horses dreamed on their feet and the wild animals, crouching to leap even in their sleep, seemed to be collecting gloom under their skins which would break out later.

On one of these days a young wolf escaped. The circus proprietor kept quiet about it, to avoid spreading alarm, but the wolf soon started raiding cattle in the neighbourhood. People at first believed that the wolf had been driven to these parts by the prospect of a severe winter, but the circus soon became suspect. The proprietor could not conceal the loss of the animal from his own employees, so the truth was bound to come out before long. The circus people offered their aid in tracking down the beast to the burgomasters of the neighbouring villagers, but all their efforts were in vain. Eventually the circus was openly blamed for the damage and the danger, and spectators stayed away.

The bound man went on performing before half-empty seats without losing anything of his amazing freedom of movement. During the day he wandered among the surrounding hills under the thin-beaten silver of the autumn sky, and, whenever he could, lay down where the sun shone longest. Soon he found a place which the twilight reached last of all, and when at last it reached him he got up most unwillingly from the withered grass. In coming down the hill he had to pass through a little wood on its southern slope, and one evening he saw the gleam of two little green lights. He knew that they came from no church window, and was not for a moment under any illusion about what they were.

He stopped. The animal came towards him through the thinning foliage. He could make out its shape, the slant of its neck, its tail which swept the ground, and its receding head. If he had not been bound, perhaps he would have tried to run away, but as it was he did not even feel fear. He stood calmly with dangling arms and looked down at the wolf's bristling coat, under which the muscles played like his own underneath the rope. He thought the evening wind was still between him and the wolf when the beast sprang. The man took care to obey his rope.

Moving with the deliberate care that he had so often put to the test, he seized the wolf by the throat. Tenderness for a fellow-creature arose in him, tenderness for the upright being concealed in the four-footed. In a movement that resembled the drive of a great bird – he felt a sudden awareness that flying would be possible only if one were tied up in a special way – he flung himself at the animal and brought it to the ground. He felt a slight elation at having lost the fatal advantage of free limbs which causes men to be worsted.[1]

The freedom he enjoyed in this struggle was having to adapt every movement of his limbs to the rope that tied him – the freedom of panthers, wolves, and the wild flowers that sway in the evening breeze. He ended up lying obliquely down the slope, clasping the animal's hind legs between his own bare feet and its head between his hands. He felt the gentleness of the faded

[1] to be defeated, with a pun on *worsted*: cloth made from closely twisted yarn or thread

116

foliage stroking the back of his hands, and he felt his own grip almost effortlessly reaching its maximum, and he felt too how he was in no way hampered by the rope.

As he left the wood light rain began to fall and obscured the setting sun. He stopped for a while under the trees at the edge of the wood. Beyond the camp and the river he saw the fields where the cattle grazed, and the places where they crossed. Perhaps he would travel south with the circus after all. He laughed softly. It was against all reason. Even if he went on putting up with his joints being covered with sores, which opened and bled when he made certain movements, his clothes would not stand up much longer to the friction of the rope.

The circus proprietor's wife tried to persuade her husband to announce the death of the wolf without mentioning that it had been killed by the bound man. She said that even at the time of his greatest popularity people would have refused to believe him capable of it, and in their present angry mood, with the nights getting cooler, they would be more incredulous than ever. The wolf had attacked a group of children at play that day, and nobody would believe that it had really been killed; for the circus proprietor had many wolves, and it was easy enough for him to hang a skin on the rail and allow free entry. But he was not to be dissuaded. He thought that the announcement of the bound man's act would revive the triumphs of the summer.

That evening the bound man's movements were uncertain. He stumbled in one of his jumps, and fell. Before he managed to get up he heard some low whistles and catcalls, rather like birds calling at dawn. He tried to get up too quickly, as he had done once or twice during the summer, with the result that he tautened the rope and fell back again. He lay still to regain his calm, and listened to the boos and catcalls growing into an uproar. 'Well, bound man, and how did you kill the wolf?' they shouted, and 'Are you the man who killed the wolf?' If he had been one of them he would not have believed it himself. He thought they had a perfect right to be angry: a circus at this time of year, a bound man, an escaped wolf, and all ending up with this. Some groups of spectators started arguing with others, but the greater part of the audience thought the whole thing a bad joke. By the time he had got to his feet there was such a hubbub that he was barely able to make out individual words.

He saw people surging up all round him, like faded leaves raised by a whirlwind in a circular valley at the centre of which all was yet still. He thought of the golden sunsets of the last few days; and the cemetery light which lay over the blight of all that he had built up during so many nights, the gold frame which the pious hang round dark, old pictures, this sudden collapse of everything, filled him with anger.

They wanted him to repeat his battle with the wolf. He said that such a thing had no place in a circus performance, and the proprietor declared that he did not keep animals to have them slaughtered in front of an audience. But the mob stormed the ring and forced them towards the cages. The proprietor's wife made her way between the seats to the exit and managed to get round to the cages from the other side. She pushed aside the attendant whom the crowd had forced to open a cage door, but the spectators dragged her back and prevented the door from being shut.

'Aren't you the woman who used to lie with him by the river in the summer?' they called out. 'How does he hold you in his arms?' She shouted back at them that they needn't believe in the bound man if they didn't want to, they had never deserved him – painted clowns were good enough for them.

The bound man felt as if the bursts of laughter were what he had been expecting ever since early May. What had smelt so sweet all through the summer now stank. But, if they insisted, he was ready to take on all the animals in the circus. He had never felt so much at one with his rope.

Gently he pushed the woman aside. Perhaps he would travel south with them after all. He stood in the open doorway of the cage, and he saw the wolf, a strong young animal, rise to its feet, and he heard the proprietor grumbling again about the loss of his exhibits. He clapped his hands to attract the animal's attention, and when it was near enough he turned to slam the cage door. He looked the woman in the face. Suddenly he remembered the proprietor's warning to suspect of murderous intentions anyone near him who had a sharp instrument in his hand. At the same moment he felt the blade on his wrists, as cool as the water of the river in autumn, which during the last few weeks he had been barely able to stand. The rope curled up in a tangle beside him while he struggled free. He pushed the woman back, but there was no point in anything he did now. Had he been insufficiently on his guard against those who wanted to release him, against the sympathy in which they wanted to lull him? Had he lain too long on the river bank? If she had cut the cord at any other moment it would have been better than this.

He stood in the middle of the cage, and rid himself of the rope like a snake discarding its skin. It amused him to see the spectators shrinking back. Did they realise that he had no choice now? Or that fighting the wolf now would prove nothing whatever? At the same time he felt all his blood rush to his feet. He felt suddenly weak.

The rope, which fell at its feet like a snake, angered the wolf more than the entry of a stranger into its cage. It crouched to spring. The man reeled, and grabbed the pistol that hung ready at the side of the cage. Then, before anyone could stop him, he shot the wolf between the eyes. The animal reared, and touched him in falling.

On the way to the river he heard the footsteps of his pursuers – spectators, the rope-dancers, the circus proprietor, and the proprietor's wife, who persisted in the chase longer than anyone else. He hid in a clump of bushes and listened to them hurrying past, and later on streaming in the opposite direction back to the camp. The moon shone on the meadow; in that light its colour was that of both growth and death.

When he came to the river his anger died away. At dawn it seemed to him as if lumps of ice were floating in the water, and as if snow had fallen, obliterating memory.

The Replacement

by Alain Robbe-Grillet

The schoolboy stepped slightly backward and looked up towards the lowest branches. Then he took a step forward, to try to reach a branch which seemed within his grasp; he stood on tiptoes and stretched his hand as high as he could, but failed to reach it. After several fruitless efforts, he apparently gave up. He lowered his arm and merely continued to stare at something among the leaves.

Next he returned to the foot of the tree, where he took up the same position as before: his knees bent slightly, the top of his body twisted to the right, and his head bent over towards his shoulder. He still held his book satchel in his left hand. It was impossible to see the other hand, with which he was no doubt supporting himself against the tree, or his face, which was almost glued to the bark of the tree, as if to scrutinise minutely some detail about a yard and a half above the ground.

The boy had again paused in his reading aloud, but this time there must have been a period,[1] perhaps even an indentation,[2] and he gave the impression that he was making an effort to indicate the end of the paragraph. The schoolboy straightened up to inspect the bark of the tree higher up.

Whispers could be heard in the classroom. The

[1] full stop
[2] space

schoolmaster turned his head and noticed that most of the pupils were looking up, instead of following the oral reading in their books; even the one reading aloud kept looking towards the teacher's desk with a vaguely questioning, or fearful, expression. The teacher said severely:

'What are you waiting for?'

The faces were all lowered silently and the boy began again, with the same studious voice, expressionless and a bit too slow, that gave each word equal emphasis and spaced it evenly from the next:

'Therefore, that evening, Joseph de Hagen, one of Philippe's lieutenants, went to the Archbishop's palace on the pretext of paying a courtesy call. As previously stated the two brothers ... '

On the other side of the street, the schoolboy peered again at the leaves on the low branches. The teacher slapped on the desk with the flat of his hand:

'As previously stated, *comma*, the two brothers ... '

Searching out the passage in his own book, he read aloud, exaggerating the punctuation:

'Start at: "As previously stated, the two brothers were already there, so that they might, if need be, protect themselves with this alibi ... " and pay attention to what you are reading.'

'As previously stated, the two brothers were already there, so that they might, if need be, protect themselves with this alibi – a suspect alibi in truth, but the best available to them at this juncture – without allowing their mistrustful cousin ... '

The monotonous voice stopped abruptly, in the middle of the sentence. The other pupils, already raising their eyes towards the paper puppet hanging on the wall, immediately returned to their books. The teacher turned his glance from the window back to the

122

boy who was reading aloud, on the opposite side of the room, in the first row near the door.

'All right, go on! There isn't any period there. You don't seem to understand what you are reading!'

The boy looked at the teacher, and behind him, slightly to the right, the puppet made of white paper.

'Do you understand or not?'

'Yes,' said the boy without much conviction.

'Yes, *sir*,' the teacher corrected him.

'Yes, sir,' the boy repeated.

The teacher looked at the printed text and asked:

'What does the word "alibi" mean to you?'

The boy looked at the puppet cut out of paper, then at the blank wall, straight in front of him, then at the book lying on his desk; and then again at the wall, for almost a full minute.

'Well?'

'I don't know, sir,' said the boy.

The teacher slowly looked over the other pupils in the class. One boy raised his hand, near the window in the back. The teacher pointed at him, and the boy stood up alongside his bench:

'It's to make people think they were there, sir.'

'Just what do you mean? Who are *they*?'

'The two brothers, sir.'

'Where did they want people to think they were?'

'At the Archbishop's, sir.'

'And where were they really?'

The boy thought for a moment before answering.

'But they were really there, sir, only they wanted to go somewhere else and make people think they were still there.'

Late at night, hidden under black masks and wrapped in huge capes, the two brothers slid down a long rope ladder into a small, deserted street.

The teacher nodded slightly a couple of times, as if he were giving his half-hearted approval. After several seconds, he said: 'Right.'

'Now you will summarise for us the whole reading passage, for the benefit of your friends who may not have understood.'

The boy looked out of the window. Then he glanced down at his book, then up again towards the teacher's desk.

'Where should I start, sir?'

'Start at the beginning of the chapter.'

Without sitting down, the boy leafed through the pages of his book and, after a short silence, began to summarise the conspiracy of Philippe de Cobourg. In spite of frequent stops and starts, he did it almost coherently. On the other hand, he stressed unduly a number of secondary matters, while hardly mentioning, or even omitting, certain crucial events. As, moreover, he was disposed to dwell on actions rather than on their political motives, it would have been extremely difficult for an uninformed listener to puzzle out the reasons for the episode or the connections between the various events described, or between the different people involved. The teacher allowed his glance to travel gradually along the windows. The schoolboy had returned to the spot below the lowest tree branch; he had put his satchel at the foot of the tree and was jumping up and down, stretching one arm upward. Seeing that all his attempts were in vain, he again stood motionless, staring at the inaccessible leaves. Philippe de Cobourg had set up camp with his mercenaries on the banks of the Neckar. The pupils, who were no longer required to follow the printed text, had all raised their heads and were silently staring at the paper puppet hanging on the wall. He had no hands or feet, but only four crudely cut-out limbs and a round head, oversized, through which ran the supporting thread. Several inches higher, at the other end of the thread, could be seen the little ball of chewed-up blotting paper that held it on the wall.

But the boy who was reciting was losing his way among wholly insignificant details, so that the teacher finally stopped him:

'That's enough,' he said, 'we know enough about that. Sit down and we will take up the reading again at the top of the page: "But Philippe and his followers . . . "'

The whole class, as one, leaned over the desks, and a new reader began, in a voice as devoid of expression as his classmate's, although conscientiously indicating the commas and the periods:

'But Philippe and his followers were not of this opinion. If the majority of the Diet – or even only the barons' party – were to renounce in this manner the prerogatives accorded to them, to him as well as to them, as a result of the invaluable assistance they had given to the Archduke's cause at the time of the uprising, they would be henceforth unable, either they or he, to demand the indictment of any new suspect, or the suspension without trial of his manorial rights. It was absolutely essential that these negotiations, which seemed to him to have begun so inauspiciously for his own cause, be broken off before the fateful date. Therefore, that evening, Joseph de Hagen, one of Philippe's lieutenants, went to the Archbishop's palace on the pretext of paying a courtesy call. As previously stated, the two brothers were already there . . . '

The faces remained dutifully leaning over the desks. The teacher looked at the window. The schoolboy was leaning against the tree, absorbed in his examination of the bark. He crouched down slowly, as if to follow a line running down the trunk – on the side not visible from the school windows. About a yard and a half above the ground, his movement stopped and he tilted his head to one side, in the same position he had formerly occupied. One by one, the faces in the classroom looked up.

The pupils looked at the teacher, then at the windows. But the bottom panes were of frosted glass, and, above, they could see only the treetops and the sky. Not a fly or a butterfly appeared on the windowpanes. Soon all eyes were again fixed on the white paper cutout of a man.

The Three Hermits

by Leo Tolstoy

AN OLD LEGEND CURRENT IN THE VOLGA DISTRICT

'And in praying use not vain repetitions, as the Gentiles do: for they think that they shall be heard for their much speaking. Be not therefore like unto them: for your Father knoweth what things ye have need of, before ye ask him.'

Matthew 6: 7–8

A bishop was sailing from Archangel to the Solovetsk Monastery, and on the same vessel were a number of pilgrims on their way to visit the shrines at that place. The voyage was a smooth one. The wind favourable and the weather fair. The pilgrims lay on deck, eating, or sat in groups talking to one another. The Bishop, too, came on deck, and as he was pacing up and down he noticed a group of men standing near the prow and listening to a fisherman, who was pointing to the sea and telling them something. The Bishop stopped, and looked in the direction in which the man was pointing. He could see nothing, however, but the sea glistening in the sunshine. He drew nearer to listen, but when the man saw him, he took off his cap and was silent. The rest of the people also took off their caps and bowed.

'Do not let me disturb you, friends,' said the Bishop. 'I came to hear what this good man was saying.'

'The fisherman was telling us about the hermits,' replied one, a tradesman, rather bolder than the rest.

'What hermits?' asked the Bishop, going to the side of the vessel and seating himself on a box. 'Tell me about them. I should like to hear. What were you pointing at?'

'Why, that little island you can just see over there,' answered the man, pointing to a spot ahead and a little to the right. 'That is the island where the hermits live for the salvation of their souls.'

'Where is the island?' asked the Bishop. 'I see nothing.'

'There, in the distance, if you will please look along my hand. Do you see that little cloud? Below it, and a bit to the left, there is just a faint streak. That is the island.'

The Bishop looked carefully, but his unaccustomed eyes could make out nothing but the water shimmering in the sun.

'I cannot see it,' he said. 'But who are the hermits that live there?'

'They are holy men,' answered the fisherman. 'I had long heard tell of them, but never chanced to see them myself till the year before last.'

And the fisherman related how once, when he was out fishing, he had been stranded at night upon that island, not knowing where he was. In the morning, as he wandered about the island, he came across an earth hut, and met an old man standing near it. Presently two others came out, and after having fed him and dried his things, they helped him mend his boat.

'And what are they like?' asked the Bishop.

'One is a small man and his back is bent. He wears a priest's cassock and is very old; he must be more than a hundred, I should say. He is so old that the white of his beard is taking a greenish tinge, but he is always smiling, and his face is as bright as an angel's from heaven. The second is taller, but he also is very old. He wears a tattered, peasant coat. His beard is broad, and of a yellowish-grey colour. He is a strong man. Before I had time to help him, he turned my boat over as if it were only a pail. He too is kindly and cheerful. The third is tall, and has a beard as white as snow and reaching to his knees. He is stern, with overhanging eyebrows; and he wears nothing but a piece of matting tied round his waist.'

'And did they speak to you?' asked the Bishop.

'For the most part they did everything in silence, and spoke but little even to one another. One of them would just give a glance, and the others would understand him. I asked the tallest whether they had lived there long. He frowned, and muttered something as if he were angry; but the oldest one took his hand and smiled, and then the tall one was quiet. The oldest one only said: "Have mercy upon us," and smiled.'

While the fisherman was talking, the ship had drawn nearer to the island.

'There, now you can see it plainly, if your Lordship will please to look,' said the tradesman, pointing with his hand.

The Bishop looked, and now he really saw a dark streak – which was the island. Having looked at it a while, he left the prow of the vessel, and going to the stern, asked the helmsman:

'What island is that?'

'That one,' replied the man, 'has no name. There are many such in this sea.'

'Is it true that there are hermits who live there for the salvation of their souls?'

'So it is said, your Lordship, but I don't know if it's true. Fishermen say they have seen them; but of course they may only be spinning yarns.'

'I should like to land on the island and see these men,' said the Bishop. 'How could I manage it?'

'The ship cannot get close to the island,' replied the helmsman, 'but you might be rowed there in a boat. You had better speak to the captain.'

The captain was sent for and came.

'I should like to see these hermits,' said the Bishop. 'Could I not be rowed ashore?'

The captain tried to dissuade him.

'Of course it could be done,' said he, 'but we should lose much time. And if I might venture to say so to your Lordship, the old men are not worth your pains. I have heard say that they are foolish old fellows, who understand nothing, and never speak a word, any more than the fish in the sea.'

'I wish to see them,' said the Bishop, 'and I will pay you for your trouble and loss of time. Please let me have a boat.'

There was no help for it; so the order was given. The sailors trimmed the sails, the steersman put up the helm, and the ship's course was set for the island. A chair was placed at the prow for the Bishop, and he sat there, looking ahead. The passengers all collected at the prow, and gazed at the island. Those who had the sharpest eyes could presently make out the rocks on it, and then a mud hut was seen. At last one man saw the hermits themselves. The captain brought a telescope and, after looking through it, handed it to the Bishop.

'It's right enough. There are three men standing on the shore. There, a little to the right of that big rock.'

The Bishop took the telescope, got it into position, and he saw the three men: a tall one, a shorter one, and one very small and bent, standing on the shore and holding each other by the hand.

The captain turned to the Bishop.

'The vessel can get no nearer in than this, your Lordship. If you wish to go ashore, we must ask you to go in the boat, while we anchor here.'

The cable was quickly let out; the anchor cast, and the sails furled. There was a jerk, and the vessel shook. Then, a boat having been lowered, the oarsmen jumped in, and the Bishop descended the ladder and took his seat. The men pulled at their oars and the boat moved rapidly towards the island. When they came within a stone's throw, they saw three old men: a tall one with only a piece of matting tied round his waist: a shorter one in a tattered peasant coat, and a very old one bent with age and wearing an old cassock – all three standing hand in hand.

The oarsmen pulled in to the shore, and held on with the boathook while the Bishop got out.

The old men bowed to him, and he gave them his blessing, at which they bowed still lower. Then the Bishop began to speak to them.

'I have heard,' he said, 'that you, godly men, live here saving your own souls and praying to our Lord Christ for your fellow men. I, an unworthy servant of Christ, am called, by God's mercy, to keep and teach his flock. I wished to see you, servants of God, and to do what I can to teach you, also.'

The old men looked at each other smiling, but remained silent.

'Tell me,' said the Bishop, 'what you are doing to save your souls, and how you serve God on this island.'

The second hermit sighed, and looked at the oldest, the very ancient one. The latter smiled, and said:

'We do not know how to serve God. We only serve and support ourselves, servant of God.'

'But how do you pray to God?' asked the Bishop.

'We pray in this way,' replied the hermit. 'Three are ye, three are we, have mercy upon us.'

And when the old man said this, all three raised their eyes to heaven, and repeated:

'Three are ye, three are we, have mercy upon us!'

The Bishop smiled.

'You have evidently heard something about the Holy Trinity,' said he. 'But you do not pray aright. You have won my affection, godly men. I see you wish to please the Lord, but you do not know how to serve him. That is not the way to pray; but listen to me, and I will teach you. I will teach you, not a way of my own, but the way in which God in the Holy Scriptures has commanded all men to pray to him.'

And the Bishop began explaining to the hermits how God had revealed himself to men; telling them of God the Father, and God the Son, and God the Holy Ghost.

'God the Son came down on earth,' said he, 'to save men, and this is how he taught us all to pray. Listen, and repeat after me: "Our Father."'

And the first old man repeated after him, 'Our Father', and the second said, 'Our Father', and the third said, 'Our Father.'

'Which art in heaven,' continued the Bishop.

The first hermit repeated, 'Which art in heaven', but the second blundered over the words, and the tall hermit could not say them properly. His hair had grown over his mouth so that he could not speak plainly. The very old hermit, having no teeth, also mumbled indistinctly.

The Bishop repeated the words again, and the old men repeated them after him. The Bishop sat down on a stone, and the old men stood before him, watching his mouth, and repeating the words as he uttered them. And all day long the Bishop laboured, saying a word twenty, thirty, a hundred times over, and the old men repeated it after him. They blundered, and he corrected them, and made them begin again.

The Bishop did not leave off till he had taught them

the whole of the Lord's Prayer so that they could not only repeat it after him, but could say it by themselves. The middle one was the first to know it, and to repeat the whole of it alone. The Bishop made him say it again and again, and at last the others could say it too.

It was getting dark and the moon was appearing over the water, before the Bishop rose to return to the vessel. When he took leave of the old men they all bowed down to the ground before him. He raised them, and kissed each of them, telling them to pray as he had taught them. Then he got into the boat and returned to the ship.

And as he sat in the boat and was rowed to the ship he could hear the three voices of the hermits loudly repeating the Lord's Prayer. As the boat drew near the vessel their voices could no longer be heard, but they could still be seen in the moonlight, standing as he had left them on the shore, the shortest in the middle, the tallest on the right, the middle one on the left. As soon as the Bishop had reached the vessel and got on board, the anchor was weighed and the sails unfurled. The wind filled them and the ship sailed away, and the Bishop took a seat in the stern and watched the island they had left. For a time he could still see the hermits, but presently they disappeared from sight, though the island was still visible. At last it too vanished, and only the sea was to be seen, rippling in the moonlight.

The pilgrims lay down to sleep, and all was quiet on deck. The Bishop did not wish to sleep, but sat alone at the stern, gazing at the sea where the island was no longer visible, and thinking of the good old men. He thought how pleased they had been to learn the Lord's Prayer; and he thanked God for having sent him to teach and help such godly men.

So the Bishop sat, thinking, and gazing at the sea

where the island had disappeared. And the moonlight flickered before his eyes, sparkling, now here, now there, upon the waves. Suddenly he saw something white and shining, on the bright path which the moon cast across the sea. Was it a seagull, or the little gleaming sail of some small boat? The Bishop fixed his eyes on it, wondering.

'It must be a boat sailing after us,' thought he, 'but it is overtaking us very rapidly. It was far, far away a minute ago, but now it is much nearer. It cannot be a boat, for I can see no sail; but whatever it may be, it is following us and catching us up.'

And he could not make out what it was. Not a boat, nor a bird, nor a fish! It was too large for a man, and besides a man could not be out there in the midst of the sea. The Bishop rose, and said to the helmsman:

'Look there, what is that, my friend? What is it?' the Bishop repeated, though he could now see plainly what it was – the three hermits running upon the water, all gleaming white, their grey beards shining, and approaching the ship as quickly as though it were not moving.

The steersman looked, and let go the helm in terror.

'Oh Lord! The hermits are running after us on the water as though it were dry land!'

The passengers, hearing him, jumped up and crowded to the stern. They saw the hermits coming along hand in hand, and the two outer ones beckoning the ship to stop. All three were gliding along upon the water without moving their feet. Before the ship could be stopped, the hermits had reached it, and raising their heads, all three as with one voice, began to say:

'We have forgotten your teaching, servant of God. As long as we kept repeating it we remembered, but when we stopped saying it for a time, a word dropped out, and now it has all gone to pieces. We can remember nothing of it. Teach us again.'

The Bishop crossed himself, and leaning over the ship's side, said:

'Your own prayer will reach the Lord, men of God. It is not for me to teach you. Pray for us sinners.'

And the Bishop bowed low before the old men; and they turned and went back across the sea. And a light shone until daybreak on the spot where they were lost to sight.

Study activities

ENCOUNTERS

The French Exchange   (United Kingdom)

1 By the end of the story, Anna 'did not feel the same at all'. How has she changed during the story? You might devise a table or chart to show your ideas.

2 Anna and Jean-Paul seem complete opposites. Make a two-column table showing their differences – in attitude, behaviour and interest. Then discuss why Jean-Paul makes such a powerful impression upon Anna by the end of the story.

3 What can we tell of the values and lifestyle of Anna and her parents? Look at their lifestyle, possessions, friends and way of talking. What do you think Lively encourages us to admire; what does she want us to question? How can you tell?

4 As she looks back on her day, what do you think Anna will think about? Write either a diary entry or monologue in which she reflects on the events, how she has changed her opinions, and how she now feels about who she is.

Cousin Rosa   (Spain)

1 What is the basic story-line in this tale? Discuss what happens.

2 Examine the characters of the narrator and Cousin Rosa. Using a two-column table, show how they differ and how they are similar. Then use it to discuss why in some ways they are attracted to one another.

3 Focus on the ending of the story – the last seven paragraphs. Which of these explanations is closest to your understanding of the ending?

- It is a realistic ending: Rosa has been caught by the narrator's fishing hook and injured.

- The ending is more symbolic: the narrator and Rosa have been strongly attracted to each other without realising it.

- The ending is like a fable, showing how the early dislike between the two characters is overpowered by an instinct of physical attraction.

- The ending doesn't 'mean' anything: it simply gives a mysterious twist to the story.

4 Look back over the story and, from a second reading, note all the hints about what is going to happen between the narrator and Rosa. Then write a detailed character study of the narrator, showing how he changes.

The Black Dog   (Netherlands)

1 The story begins with an April Fool's Day prank. Why is the incident so important to the boy? Why do you think he reacts so angrily? Discuss his behaviour at this point.

2 We do not learn the names of either the boy himself, his mother or his father. What do we know of their characters by the end of the story? Make a list for each character of what he or she is like. Make connections showing similarities and differences between them.

3 The boy watches his father being attacked by the black dog. 'Run. Go home. Hurry up,' his father commands him. Discuss whether you think the boy was right to obey this order. Why do you think he did run home? Would you have done the same?

4 Discuss why you think the boy twice reflects on the 'picture from the time he had not yet existed'. What does it show us about the boy's character and his attitude to his parents?

5 Create a dialogue between the mother and father in the story, in which they discuss the events which took place that day and reflect on the way their son has reacted.

A Vendetta   (France)

1 When the widow Saverini sees the body of her murdered only son, she 'did not weep, but stood for some time, without moving, staring down at him'. What is going through her mind at this point? Bearing in mind that she quickly swears to be avenged, work in pairs to create a monologue expressing what she is thinking. Then perform it directly to the class or on to video.

2 There seem to be no clues about why the son was murdered. Is this a weakness in the story, or a clue as to why widow Saverini feels so determined to gain revenge? Discuss the possibilities.

3 Discuss why you think widow Saverini disguises herself as a man in order to avenge her son's murder.

4 Imagine how a local newspaper might report the murder of Nicolas Ravolati. Write the front page story, perhaps including speculation about who the murderer might have been.

5 Imagine that widow Saverini is put on trial for the murder of Nicolas Ravolati. Write her speech defending her action, arguing the justice of her case.

Big Fish, Little Fish   (Italy)

1 'A sea-bed is lovely the first time one discovers it.' Discuss Zeffirino's attitude to the natural world: does he admire, celebrate, enjoy, ignore or destroy it? Look for evidence in the story.

2 Look at the character of Signorina De Magistris. What is she like at the beginning of the story? What is *her* attitude to nature? How has she changed by the end of the story, if at all? You might devise a chart to show any character development.

3 Discuss the way Calvino presents men and women. Do you notice strong differences between the portrayal of the sexes? Make a two-column list to show your observations.

4 Rewrite the story from Signorina De Magistris's point of view, either as a narrative or as a diary. What different perceptions does she bring to the day's events?

ENCOUNTERS: the five stories

• Compare the encounters which take place in two or three of the stories in this section. What different effects do they have on the participants? Are the encounters positive or negative? How do different characters react and change as a result?

- Which of the stories in this section did you find most and least enjoyable? Write about your response.

- Did any of the stories feel obviously translated? Did the language feel unusual or distant in any way? Write about your response to the language used in one of the stories.

STRANGE TALES

The White Woman   (Austria)

1 Look back at the character of the man. Make two lists: one showing what we learn about him in the story (interests, appearance, behaviour, thoughts), the other showing what we do not learn but wonder about. Then use the points in your list to discuss the way we respond to his character – how interesting, likeable and sympathetic do we find him?

2 Who or what is the White Woman? Look again at the mysterious words she speaks. What theories do you have about who she might be? Discuss these in a small group.

3 Retell the story from the point of view of one of the servants – hearing the old man's voice, going into the room, describing the way he reacts. Give your account of the strange event. What do you think is going on?

4 This is a strange story which leaves the reader wondering what actually happened. Write a personal response, describing your reactions – to the plot, characters, the place and the use of language.

The Elephant (Poland)

1 The first sentence of the story tells us about the Director of the Zoological Gardens. What do we learn about him during the course of the story? Consider his behaviour, language, attitude to staff and opinions. Are we shown anything *positive* about him?

2 As in some other stories in this collection (for example *The White Woman*), we are given none of the names of the characters. Nor are we shown anything about their physical appearance or backgrounds. In a group, discuss these statements and decide which you most agree with:

- The lack of realistic details makes the story move along faster.

- We concentrate more upon the story-line than the characters.

- It gives the story the feel of a fairy-tale rather than a realistic, believable story.

- It prevents us from becoming involved in the events of the story.

3 Look back to the start of the story. At which precise point did you realise that it was not going to be a realistic tale?

4 This story was written in 1957. At the start of World War II, in 1939, Poland was divided between Germany and Soviet Russia. At the end of the war a 'people's republic' was established, with Poland kept under close Soviet supervision. Opposition to the oppression of Stalin led to civil unrest in 1956, serious strikes and riots.

How important do you think knowing about the political background is in fully understanding this story? Discuss any possible 'message' the story might have. Are there other stories in this collection in which you feel you would like to know more about the historical context?

5 Write a letter of complaint from the schoolteacher who takes his class to see the elephant. Explain what happened during the visit, how you and your class reacted to the disappearance of the elephant, and what happened next. Address your letter either to the Director of the Zoo, or to one of the 'soulless' officials in Warsaw.

Unexpected Guests   (Germany)

1 Discuss the character of the narrator and, in particular, examine his attitude to his wife and children. How sympathetic do you find him?

2 Do you find the story amusing, or does it become too far-fetched for your taste? If so, at which point do you think the story becomes too absurd?

3 Imagine you are one of the family's neighbours. Create a role-play or dialogue in which you confront them to complain about the noise and smell of their animals.

4 Imagine that an even more unexpected guest arrives at the house – say, a giraffe or gorilla. Continue the story to show what happens next.

'Oof,' he said.   (Spain)

1 What kind of people are the two characters of the story? Look again at the details we are given about them (their conversation, their card-game, their watching of television), and what happens while they sleep. What do all these details suggest about them?

2 Quim Monzo has a powerful and poetic writing style. For example he writes: 'She let the teaspoon drop on to the table with a gentle, soft, orange-coloured sound.' Discuss what this might mean, and pick out some other examples of his images which you find striking.

3 The ending of the story echoes the beginning. What do you think will happen next? Discuss the possibilities.

4 Write a story in which little happens and yet we learn a lot about the characters. Use language to give a strong sense of place and dialogue, and don't feel that you have to move to any clear conclusion – make the written style the main focus. A starting-point might be to decide upon a setting for the narrative.

Jennifer's Dreams (Germany)

1 What category of story is this? Discuss which of these labels feels most appropriate: thriller, suspense story, mystery, ghost story, family drama, children's story.

2 Discuss how far you agree with one reader's comments:

> The story is called *Jennifer's Dreams* but it's not really about Jennifer at all. It's about the way her parents are drifting apart and the effect this is having upon Jennifer. Her dreams stop when her parents finally stop competing with each other.

3 Find examples in the story of the way Jennifer's dreams are echoed in the real events that take place. How do you explain her dreams?

4 How would the story have worked if it had been written as a first-person narrative from Jennifer's point of view? Take the first page or so of the story and rewrite it in this style. Then explain the different effect you have created.

STRANGE TALES: the five stories

- Which of these stories seemed to you the most strange? What made it unusual – the behaviour of the characters, the writer's style, the ending? Discuss your reaction.

MODERN FABLES

The Blue Jar   (Denmark)

1 This story begins 'There was once . . .', making it feel like a fairy-tale. Make a list of any other signs that this story belongs to that genre. In particular look at the characters, events, ending and language.

2 As well as details from the past the story contains references to the present. Make a list, in two columns, of five details from the past and five from the present. Then discuss what effect this has upon the story as a whole.

3 Discuss what the moral of the story might be.

4 Many readers will be concerned at the way this story portrays Lady Helena. Look at these comments from one reader:

> Lady Helena is shown as weak and passive. She throws her life away hunting something pointless and is shown to be at the mercy of the men in her life rather than in control of her own fate.

Do you agree with this assessment of the story? Are there

arguments against this opinion? How would the story work if the central character were male?

5 Write a version of the story reversing the gender of the characters – the old Englishman becomes a woman; she is accompanied by her son rather than daughter, and so on.

6 Write a response to the story discussing what you liked or did not like about it, your response to the characters and plot, and the qualities of fairy-tale which the story has.

Seven Floors (Italy)

1 Trace the way the personality of Giovanni Corte alters as he is told of each new change of floor. How is he different at the end of the story from the beginning?

2 Discuss how you responded to the story as you read it. At which point did you realise it was inevitable that Corte would finally be placed on the first floor?

3 We learn little about the staff of the hospital, often not even doctors' names. Discuss the effect this has.

4 What do you think happens next? Write a continuation of the story showing what happens to Giovanni Corte.

5 Write a comparison of *Seven Floors* with one of the other stories which shows humans made helpless, for example *The Bound Man*. Compare their central characters, what happens to them and the way the writers show them struggling to remain individuals.

The Bound Man   (Austria)

1 At the beginning of the story the bound man seeks freedom; by the end he 'had never felt so much at one with his rope'. Discuss the effect being bound by rope has upon him and the way he changes during the story.

2 Discuss the way in which the attitude of the circus proprietor's wife differs from her husband's attitude to the bound man. How do they both view him?

3 At the end of the story, when he has been freed, the man feels anger. Discuss what you think he is angry about – being bound, being released, or the attitudes of the villagers?

4 Now physically free again, what does the bound man think of his period tied up? Write a diary entry or monologue in which he reflects upon the effect of being bound in ropes.

5 A number of the stories in this collection use unusual situations to show something about human society – think, for example, of Slawomir Mrozek's *The Elephant*, which shows the stifling effect of bureaucracy. Write a reflective essay exploring what *The Bound Man* might symbolise about human beings' need for freedom and restraint.

The Replacement   (France)

1 This is one of the strangest stories in this collection. To help untangle its meaning look more closely at the two story-lines which are going on. Discuss: What happens *in* the classroom? What happens *outside* the classroom? How are the events of these two story-lines linked?

2 What do you think the story 'means'? Look at these comments and discuss which, if any, you agree with:

- 'The story shows how pointless this kind of education is – all the teacher seems concerned about is the way his students read the punctuation marks, not the content of the text itself.'

- 'The story shows how unnatural schooling can be – that is why the boy outside the window is "absorbed in his examination of the bark" of the tree: it shows that he, unlike the people in the classroom, is in tune with nature.'

- 'The story is encouraging readers to be individuals, rather than doing simply what is required of us.'

- 'The story does not blame anyone for this deadly lesson: it simply shows us that this is what "systems" do – they sap the life out of things.'

For each quotation that you agree with, try to find evidence from the text to support the statement. What other statements would you add to summarise the story?

3 Discuss why you think the story is called *The Replacement*.

4 What do you think happens next, both inside the classroom and outside? Continue the story, either in short story form, or as a role-play or script.

5 'Schools are rarely shown positively in literature.' Do you agree with this statement? From your reading of three or four different texts, write an essay about the portrayal of schools, teachers and pupils.

The Three Hermits   (Russia)

1 Tolstoy gives his story the subtitle 'An old legend'. Read this dictionary definition and then discuss what elements this story has which makes it a legend:

> A popular story handed down from earlier times whose truth has not been ascertained; a modern story that has taken on the characteristics of a traditional legendary tale; a story of the life of a saint. (*Collins English Dictionary*)

Are there any further ingredients you would expect in a legend? Does Tolstoy's story also contain these?

2 Are we supposed to like the central character of the bishop, or is he unsympathetic? Debate his character, deciding what you think Tolstoy wants us to think of him, and supporting your ideas with evidence from the text.

3 Discuss what you think is the moral of the tale.

4 How difficult did you find the language of this story, written in 1886? Is the translation clear and attractive? Write a version for a younger audience, for example primary school pupils. Then write a brief commentary saying what you altered in the story, what problems you encountered and how well you think your new translation works.

5 Write your own legendary story, perhaps based upon a poem you have read. Look, for example, at Philip Larkin's 'The North Ship' or Walter de la Mare's 'The Listeners', and create a prose narrative based upon it.

MODERN FABLES: the five stories

- Which of the stories in this section had the most powerful effect upon you? Discuss what you liked about it.

- Which story had language which felt unusual or distant? Did you enjoy the writer's use of language? Write about your response, giving examples from the text.

- Which of the stories in this section did you find most and least enjoyable? Write about your response.

The authors

Ilse Aichinger (1921–   ) was born in Vienna, where she studied medicine after the war, and worked for a publishing company, reading manuscripts of new authors. She then became a novelist, for which she has received several major Austrian prizes for literature.

J. Bernlef (1937–   ) lives in Amsterdam and began to write in 1960. He has since written around fifty books – poems, novels, essays and plays – and his work has won numerous prestigious prizes. He says of *The Black Dog* that it deals with 'one of the cornerstones of literature': the discovery of lies.

Heinrich Böll (1917–85) was one of Germany's most famous and influential novelists. The political injustice and cruelty he witnessed in his youth and during military service in Nazi Germany form the basis of much of his writing. In 1972 he won the Nobel Prize for Literature, a major international award.

Dino Buzzati (1906–72) was born and lived in northern Italy, where he worked as a journalist and wrote about his wide-ranging interests in politics, science and the arts, as well as UFO sightings. In his fiction, he experimented with a range of forms – science-fiction, parables, fairy-tales, dreams and fantasies. He was also a painter.

Italo Calvino (1923–85) grew up in San Remo, Italy. He was the son of a curator of botanical gardens and his stories often centre around the magic of the living world. He was the author of many short stories, novels and essays, and enjoyed experimenting with ways of telling stories.

Isak Dinesen (1885–1962). This is a pseudonym for the Danish writer Karen Blixen, best known for her memoir, *Out of Africa*, which was also a highly successful film. After a seventeen-year period living in East Africa, she returned to Denmark to write stories, usually in English. In the late 1950s she was repeatedly named as the leading candidate for the Nobel Prize in Literature, but she was never awarded it.

Marie Luise Kaschnitz (1901–74) became well-known as a poet as well as a fiction writer. She later wrote radio plays and essays. She was at one time visiting Professor of Aesthetics at Frankfurt University in Germany.

Penelope Lively (1933–   ) grew up in Egypt but settled in England after the war and studied history at Oxford. She is well-known for her children's fiction, for example *The Ghost of Thomas Kempe*. Since 1977 she has been writing for adults, with considerable success. In 1987 she won the Booker Prize for Fiction for her novel *Moon Tiger*.

Guy de Maupassant (1850–93) was born into a cultured, middle-class family. When the Franco-Prussian War destroyed the family finances in 1870, he began to earn a living as a minor civil servant in Paris. Here, encouraged by the great French novelist Flaubert, he began writing. In a ten-year period from 1880, he wrote about 300 short stories, 200 newspaper articles, 6 novels and 3 travel books. He died insane at the age of 42.

José María Merino (1941–   ) was born in La Coruña in north-west Spain and later settled in Madrid. He has written poetry, travel books, novels and numerous short stories. He has also produced a trilogy of books specifically for young people.

Quim Monzo (1952–   ) has had a varied career – cartoonist, movie scriptwriter, graphic designer and war correspondent. He has published novels, short stories and collections of journalism. He writes in Catalan, the language of the north-eastern region of Spain, an area of strongly independent traditions. His work has all been translated into Spanish.

Slawomir Mrozek (1930–   ) is best known in his native Poland as a playwright. His work was banned there until a more liberal phase began in the 1970s. Translator Konrad Syrop says that 'most of Mrozek's work can be read and interpreted on at least two levels' – partly as a story, partly as a political parable.

Alain Robbe-Grillet (1922–   ) is a French writer with an international reputation. His concept of the *nouveau roman* radically rejected traditional elements of the novel - characterisation, plot, narrative - and instead tried to present reality through a series of impressions. He has also directed films.

Arthur van Schendel (1874–1946) was a Dutch novelist, poet and short story writer. He was fascinated by writing 'naturalist fiction' – stories which show the everyday details of ordinary people's lives. His story *The White Woman* was written in 1938.

Leo Tolstoy (1828–1910). The youngest of four brothers, Count Leo Nikolayevich Tolstoy was born in Tula province, about one hundred miles south of Moscow. He served in the army in the Crimean War (1853–6), returning home to write short stories and novels such as *War and Peace*. He became one of the most popular writers in Russia, and was renowned for his science fiction and adventure novels. Nowadays he is remembered chiefly for his long and hugely ambitious historical novels.

Further reading

General collections

The Penguin Book of International Short Stories edited by
Daniel Halpern (Penguin, 1989)
A huge collection of stories, many from Europe, but the
majority from North and South America. The book
represents a survey of post-war international short stories.

The Virago Book of Fairy Tales edited by Angela Carter
(Virago, 1991)
A useful book to see other, older traditions of short stories,
legends and fables.

The Origins of Desire edited by Juan Antonio Masoliver
(Serpent's Tail, 1993)
A lively collection of contemporary Spanish short stories.

The Dedalus Book of Dutch Fantasy edited by Richard Huijing
(Dedalus, 1993)
An anthology of dark, disturbing non-realistic tales.

The Quality of Light edited by Ann and Michael Caesar
(Serpent's Tail, 1993)
Contemporary short stories from Italy.

Sudden Fiction International edited by Robert Shapard and
James Thomas (Paladin, 1991)
A fascinating collection from Europe and around the world
of very short stories.

Individual authors

Pack of Cards by Penelope Lively (Penguin, 1987)
A collection of short stories by this well-known writer.

The Raid and Other Stories by Leo Tolstoy (Oxford University Press, 1982)
An interesting selection of his shorter stories.

Mademoiselle Fifi and Other Stories by Guy de Maupassant (Oxford University Press, 1993)
A gripping selection from a master story-teller.

The Stories of Heinrich Böll by Heinrich Böll (Penguin, 1992)
Short and often very funny stories from one of Germany's best-known writers.

Further reading projects

1 Choose one writer whose work you have particularly enjoyed, and write an introduction to her or his work aimed at the general reader.

2 Choose a theme – such as legends, individual versus state, growing up – and compare two or more authors whose stories deal with the theme.

3 From your reading of a variety of writers from different European countries, do you notice any differences in their portrayal of people and places? Do different authors seem to write distinctively from their own country's context, or is it fairer to say that there is a general European feel? Illustrate your ideas with references to a number of writers from different countries.